HOW TO RAISE
AN OLD EN
SHEEPD

By Mona Berkowitz

Distributed in the U.S.A. by T.F.H. Publications, Inc., 211 West Sylvania Avenue, P.O. Box 27, Neptune City, N.J. 07753; in England by T.F.H. (Gt. Britain) Ltd., 13 Nutley Lane, Reigate, Surrey; in Canada to the book store and library trade by Clarke, Irwin & Company, Clarwin House, 791 St. Clair Avenue West, Toronto 10, Ontario; in Canada to the pet trade by Rolf C. Hagen Ltd., 3225 Sartelon Street, Montreal 382, Quebec; in Southeast Asia by Y.W. Ong, 9 Lorong 36 Geylang, Singapore 14; in Australia and the south Pacific by Pet Imports Pty. Ltd., P.O. Box 149, Brookvale 2100, N.S.W., Australia. Published by T.F.H. Publications, Inc. Ltd., The British Crown Colony of Hong Kong.

Cover painting by Ernest H. Hart

Frontispiece: Ch. Merriedip Duke George, owned by the Author and bred by Hope Norton. Sire: Ch. Merriedip Mister Personality; dam: Merriedip Pamela. This great dog was one of the most prominent winners in the history of the breed. Many times a best in show winner, Duke George made numerous friends for the breed and was owner-shown throughout his long, illustrious career in the ring.

Photo Credits

Evelyn Shafer, Ake Wintzell, Sport & General Press Agency, Ltd., William Brown, C. M. Cooke & Son, Percy T. Jones, Joan Ludwig, Henry C. Schley.

ISBN 0-87666-344-7

Contents

I. History, Description and Standard

BACKGROUND OF THE BREED

The first graphic evidence of the Old English Sheepdog is found in the portrait of the Duke of Buccleuch painted by Gainsborough and dated 1771. It depicts the Duke with his arm draped about his canine companion, a typical Old English of that period. Through simple arithmetic this makes the breed at least 196 years old.

It was about 1888, more than a hundred years later, that the breed was first introduced into the United States. William Wade of Hulton, Pa., and his close friend, Andrew Carnegie of Pittsburgh, Pa., were completely responsible

Int. Ch. Unnesta Pim, owned by Mr. and Mrs. Barry Goodman and bred by M. Korfitzen. Sire: Reeuwijks Cupid; dam: Int. Ch. Shepton Sally Ann. A champion in many countries, Pim has also proven his worth as a producer of top stock.

Ch. Bridal Gown, owned by Mrs. F. Gatehouse. Sire: Penzance Wallflower; dam: Colleen. This bitch was a prominent winner earlier in this century.

Ch. King's Messenger, owned by Stanley Kraft and bred by Julius Kraft. Sire: Ch. Merriedip of Pastorale; dam: Ch. Mistress Opal of Pastorale. This dog is another who excelled as a winner and producer.

Ch. Fernville Fernando, owned by Norman W. R. Harrison. Sire: Nero of Hardwickings; dam: Shepton Silver Wendy. This English winner finished to his championship at a very early age and has produced top winners both in Great Britain and in the United States.

for importing the first specimens of the breed to this country. Wade's aim was to give every American a better dog—a pedigreed dog and a dog of usefulness no matter what its country of origin.

It was William Wade's practice to deposit a Sheepdog upon the doorstep of his unsuspecting friends and neighbors, food and all. Naturally those lovable, handsome gratis gifts soon won the hearts of each household.

In 1889 Mr. Wade published the monograph *The Old English Sheepdog*, written and compiled by Freeman Lloyd; the publishing was entirely at his personal expense through *Turf, Field and Farm of New York*.

This article had tremendous impact and influence upon its readers and put into active motion the first heavy invasion of the breed into our country.

Actually the "Bob-tail" had almost become extinct in Britain. It was the American demand which stimulated the market for Old English Sheepdogs not only for export abroad but in their home country.

The finest specimens of years gone by were reared primarily in Southern England in places such as Cornwall, East England, South and South Western England. Cardiff in Wales was noted for raising the finest Sheepherding strain of the breed.

It is interesting to note that in the English Kennel Club stud book Vol. VIII of 1881 they listed the breed as "English Short Tailed Colley." To this day no one knows how the word "Colley" was tacked on to the early members of the breed. The late Freeman Lloyd wrote the first description of the Old English Sheepdog when the Old English Sheepdog Club was formed. Mr. Lloyd gave much praise to the late Dr. Edwards-Kerr whose memory of the breed embellished the original description.

The Woodbridge doctor gave much glamour and romance to the Old English Sheepdog. It was an evolution of the shepherd's rollicking, roustabout pal developing into the wealthy ladies' fondling. He has gradually transformed from an out-of-doors dog to the fancy house pet.

The first large class of Bob-tails, in America was at the Westminster Kennel Club show in 1903 judged by Mr. Lloyd, The Messrs. Tilley of Shepton Mallet, England brought a team of Old English Sheepdogs for competition at this show.

The dogs brought over for this show were eventually sold to such well known people as the late Richard Harding Davis, war correspondent and Charles Dillingham, noted New York theatrical producer. Dillingham, in time, presented some of his stock to the late Reginald G. Vanderbilt of Newport, Rhode Island. Vanderbilt in turn bred Ch. Sandy Boy Rags, the dog credited with being the progenitor of the white-headed, blue-bodied Sheepdogs which were the top winners of the early thirties.

BREEDERS, BLOODLINES AND CONTEMPORARY HISTORY

It was about this time that Mrs. Lewis Roesler (the late Mrs. Edward P. Renner) established her famed bob-tail Kennels "Merriedip" located at Great Barrington, Mass. She imported the "Pastorole" and "Downderry" blood lines. For some twenty years she bred and exhibited some of the finest in this country.

The prefix "Merriedip" has always carried with it an aura of prestige when noted in pedigrees or made reference to in bloodlines.

Champions bearing the "Merriedip" prefix numbered many and won in the show rings across the country. The most famous winner of her kennel was the breath-taking "Ch. Merriedip Master Pantaloons." His best in show, breed, and group wins made breed history in his era. Among the most treasured of his triumphs was the working group first won at the Westminster Kennel Club. He was handled by the late George MacKercher, kennel manager for "Merriedip."

Many other dedicated and enthusiastic breeders have joined the passing parade and their noble animals still exert great influence upon our modern-day dogs.

The late Hope Robinson Hitchcock with two of her fine Old English. This lady was one of many who bred top animals that paved the way for some of the great ones of modern times.

Ch. Merriedip Master Pantaloons, owned and bred by the late Mrs. E. P. Renner, with whom he is shown. Sire: Ch. Downderry Volunteer; dam: Ch. Mistress Petticoats of Pastorale. One of the standouts in breed history, this dog brought added notice to the breed by reason of his fine show record and through his many champion children.

Prominent fanciers in the United States have been Mrs. Tyler Morse, Mr. and Mrs. Morris Kinney of "Kinnelon" kennels fame. Judge and Mrs. Wilbur Kirby Hitchcock, Mr. and Mrs. William Jamison of "Willinez Weather" kennels, Mrs. Laura H. Dorhing of the Cliffwood Sheepdogs, Mrs. Roland M. Baker who established the "Woodland" kennels. Mr. and Mrs. P. Hamilton Goodsell and their son Percy were extremely active in every phase of breeding, exhibiting and exportation of dogs under the illustrious "Tenacre" kennel name.

Mrs. Doris M. Briggs gave much of her energies both as a breeder and exhibitor of Bob-tails using her "Cartref" kennel name, which was also famed for Springer Spaniels.

Mrs. Rosalind Crafts exerted much influence through her careful breeding program and quality specimens. "Rosmoore" will always be considered a quality hallmark when found in any pedigree. She will be well remembered as having had many best in show awards with her homebreds, but the most thrilling sight of all was to see her guide her Ch. Rosmoore Sinney (then 15 months of age) on to a Best In Show win. Mrs. Crafts was in her late sixties when she won this coveted award with her exhibit. As owner, handler, and breeder it was a tremendous triumph.

Marjorie and Helen Cluff of "Clearbrook" kennels exhibited one of the most outstanding and beloved sheepdogs of years gone by. As owners of their Canadian kennels they campaigned "Ch. Snowflake" to record awards.

Other breeders of the past whose influence has been strongly felt in the breed are Mrs. Mary Schloss, owner of "Mobla" kennels, Mrs. V. Cline

9

Ch. Rosmoore Joy's Gift, owned, bred, and handled by the late Mrs. C. M. Crafts. Sire: Ch. Rosmoore Smarty Pants II; dam: Rosmoore Leading Lady. At the age of fifteen months this homebred was best of opposite sex at the Old English Sheepdog Club of America Specialty under judge Dr. Donald Davidson. Below left, Mrs. Crafts is shown handling her homebred, Ch. Rosmoore Sinney to best of breed at the New England Old English Sheepdog Club under the Author. Ch. Salt Box Granny Bee, owned by Ceil Day Wood and handled here by William Trainor was awarded best of opposite sex.

Lindley, "Lynnhaven" kennels, Mrs. George Ott, "Bubbling Springs" kennels, and Mrs. Alonzo P. Walton, of "Royal" kennels. Mr. Alonzo Walton survives today and is still a member of the New England Old English Sheepdog Club.

It was in 1873 that the Old English Sheepdogs were first given separate classification at a dog show; this was in Curzon Hall, Birmingham, England.

The Old English Sheepdog Club was founded in England in 1888 and the breed grew and gained in popularity so that in 1914, there were 111 dogs benched at their Specialty Show.

The first specimen of the breed shown in the United States was "Hempstead Bob," bred by Dr. Lock, of England. This dog was owned by "Hempsted Farms" and exhibited at the Westminster Kennel Club Show in 1893. Twelve years later the Old English Sheepdog Club of America was officially founded and approved by the American Kennel Club in the year 1905. The late H. A. Tilley of England deserves full credit for the founding of the Old English Sheepdog Club of America. It was his eager spirit that, in 1904, stimulated the interested owners and breeders in America to band together to form an organized association.

Ch. Baroness of Duroya (left) owned and handled by Barry Goodman and Ch. Tara-Wood's Blue Baron, owned by the late Adeline H. Isakson and handled by Howard Tyler, were best of opposite sex and best of breed, respectively, at the Old English Sheepdog Club of America 1964 Specialty. The judge was Mrs. Mona Berkowitz.

During World War I two Old English Sheepdogs made international history. The dogs named "Haig" and "Pershing" were adopted by Madame Capehart Viseuer, head of the Marme hospital, at the tender age of 6 months. They were given rigorous training and sent off into active duty. Trained not to bark, they were sent out in the ambulances to cover the front line action searching for the dead and wounded. They constantly risked their lives in "No Man's Land." "Pershing" is said to have notified stretcher bearers of the location of over 300 wounded men. "Haig" is credited with having saved 700 lives.

"Haig" and "Pershing" toured the United States under the care and guidance of Mrs. Walter Colverd and Mrs. Amy Baruch. Two of "Haig's" sons also saw active service at the front. They were owned by Mrs. Walter Colverd of San Francisco. The photographs of Mrs. Baruch, Mrs. Colverd, "Haig" and "Pershing" were published in the Los Angeles Evening Herald shortly before the end of the war.

By the mid-thirties the breed had become well accepted and was enjoying

The celebrated canine war heroes, Haig (right) and Pershing. During World War I these dogs were responsible for the saving of hundreds of human lives. Mrs. Walter Colverd (left) and Mrs. Amy Baruch conducted a nationwide tour of the United States to introduce these dogs to the American public.

a good degree of popularity. It was at this time that a group of extremely active breeders and exhibitors in the New England States joined together to establish the New England Old English Sheepdog Club. Among its founding members were Mrs. C. M. Crafts, Mrs. Walter Roesler, Mrs. Roland M. Baker, and Miss Edith N. Buckingham.

Both clubs (the parent club and the New England club) have functioned actively over the years, growing in membership and presenting matches and specialty shows under their sponsorship in the breed's behalf. In Britain too the breed grew in numbers and fanciers. Several additional breed clubs have been organized over the years. Today there are five Breed Societies in the United Kingdom.

There is no doubt that the breed has skyrocketed in popularity in recent years. We need only to refer to the American Kennel Club registrations and records to substantiate these facts. Less than a dozen years ago the Old

Momarv's Bruno Boy Hayseed, owned by the Author and Mr. Sven Lillquist, was best in show from the classes at the San Gabriel Valley KC under judge Nelson Groh.

English Sheepdog ranked as 75th place among the hundred-odd recognized American Kennel Club breeds. In 1958 there were 106 Old English Sheepdogs registered. In 1962 the A.K.C. listed 252. The greatest increase in registrations was over the three successive years with a registration of 809 dogs recorded in 1965. The breed then was listed as 55th in a listing of 115 recognized breeds. The figures on record for 1966 show a total registration of 1,267 giving the Bob-tail a 45th place in popularity.

Certainly devotees of the breed are encouraged by the forward progress in numbers, but, like the "Ides of March," let the breeders beware! Much harm can be done by an over abundance of quantity and the goal for the future should above all be quality.

13

The three dogs on this page are all owned by Mr. and Mrs. Hendrik Van Rensselaer. At the left is Ch. Farleydene Bartholemew. Sire: Farley Rudolph; dam: Shepton Misty Light. A distinguished sire, he is pictured here with Mr. Van Rensselaer.

(right)
Ch. Fezziwig Ceiling Zero, a homebred, sired by Ch. Farleydene Bartholemew out of Patchwork Gillian. "Ceily" stands out as one of the most distinguished dogs in the history of the breed. He was one of the top winning dogs of all breeds and is the sire of eleven champions.

Ch. Fezziwig Raggedy Andy, one of the most prodigious winners the breed has ever produced. He has won best in show at some of the most important events in the U. S. Included in his triumphs are Chicago International, Trenton, Detroit and a host of others. He was twice best in the working group at the Westminster Kennel Club and was shown to these great wins by Robert S. Forsyth.

DESCRIPTION

The Old English Sheepdog, also affectionately referred to as the Bob-tail, is a rollicking, frolicksome clown with a "Peter Pan" complex inasmuch as he never greatly grows up in personality. He is a sturdy, blue and white, compact dog of good size. The ideal having been expressed in size for males (by the late A. Hopwood and H. A. Tilley both famous breeders of the past in England) as being 25 inches at the shoulder.

Size, however, is not and should never be considered as a prime factor. Quality, type, and soundness are to be considered paramount at all times.

Color must always be blue and white. Although there is no definite requirement contained in the breed standard as to how the markings shall be placed on the dogs it has been the practice of many breeders, here and abroad, to discourage the breeding and exhibiting of dogs whose blue body markings have been splashed with patches of white.

The ideal coat is actually a combination of two coats. The outer coat, extremely harsh (and may we stress wavy and free from curl), is often referred to as the guard hairs. The undercoat is of a lighter blue coloring, very dense (unless removed by excessive grooming) and rather cottony soft, but exceedingly waterproof and serves as insulation in extreme weather conditions. Blue coloring ranges from very light silver blue to a blue as deep as navy being correct, never black.

Our ideal Bob-tail has a very square skull, well arched over the eyes which should be well covered by head coat, often referred to as the "fall." Of prime importance is the proper length and arch of neck.

Proper amount and arch of neck adds to the breed's regal bearing and was a functional requirement of the true worker. The Old English Sheepdog is about the most affectionate and responsive of all dog breeds. They thrive on love, attention and when not receiving what they believe to be a sufficient quantity from their human associates will seek to let it be known by the lift of a forepaw that they indeed will not be overlooked or denied. They make the ideal family dog. Kind with children, patient and active yet sedate when these qualities are required of them.

The deep quality of their bark (referred to by the Standard as a "pot-casse" ring) is enough to recommend them as a watchdog in the home. They are not a one-man, one-family type breed however; in general they love all mankind.

The Old English Sheepdog has a fine mind and is easily trained. His records in the obedience ring speak highly of his intelligence. Many of the breed have been trained over the past 30 years to bring honor and pride to the Old English Sheepdog as successful movie and theatrical stars in their own rights.

Their record and reputation as sheepherding dogs both here and in

England has been well established. This naturally was the main and original purpose for which they were initially bred. They have been successful as cattle dogs, herders of fowl and even swine. They make an excellent retriever both on land and (when clipped down) in water. They are noted for a good nose and soft mouth when used for game.

The breed is equally adaptable and comfortable in an apartment, mansion, or typical home. He enjoys the outdoor type of life as well and has flourished as farmyard dog and herd dog. He has been successfully bred in all countries of the world including India and southern climates such as Florida and has withstood the damp and cold of Scotland and the rigors of the Alaskan cold as well.

Many times the breed has been likened in conformation to the bear. The unique ambling, rolling gait, the low set of hock and rounded rear quarters are indeed similar in appearance and structure to that of the bruin families.

STANDARD OF THE OLD ENGLISH SHEEPDOG

Skull—Capacious and rather squarely formed, giving plenty of room for brain power. The parts over the eyes should be well arched and the whole well covered with hair.

Jaw—Fairly long, strong, square and truncated. The stop should be well defined to avoid a Deerhound face. (The attention of judges is particularly called to the above properties, as a long, narrow head is a deformity.)

Eyes—Vary according to the color of the dog. Very dark preferred, but in the glaucous or blue dogs a pearl, wall or china eye is considered typical. (A light eye is most objectionable.)

Nose—Always black, large and capacious.

Teeth—Strong and large, evenly placed and level in opposition.

Ears—Medium sized, and carried flat to side of head, coated moderately.

Legs—The forelegs should be dead straight, with plenty of bone, removing the body a medium height from the ground, without approaching legginess, and well coated all around.

Feet—Small, round; toes well arched, and pads thick and hard.

Tail—It is preferable that there should be none. Should never, however, exceed one and a half or two inches in grown dogs. When not natural-born bobtails however, puppies should be docked at the first joint from the body and the operation performed when they are from three to four days old.

Neck and Shoulders—The neck should be fairly long, arched gracefully and well coated with hair. The shoulders sloping and narrow at the points, the dog standing lower at the shoulder than at the loin.

Body—Rather short and very compact, ribs well sprung and brisket deep and capacious. Slabsidedness highly undesirable. The loin should be very stout and gently arched, while the hindquarters should be round and muscular and with well let down hocks, and the hams densely coated with a thick long jacket in excess of any other part.

Coat—Profuse, but not so excessive as to give the impression of the dog being over-fat, and of a good hard texture; not straight, but shaggy and free from curl. Quality and texture of coat to be considered above mere profuseness. Softness or flatness of coat to be considered a fault. The undercoat should be a waterproof pile, when not removed by grooming or season.

Color—Any shade of gray, grizzle, blue or blue-merled with or without white markings or in reverse. Any shade of brown or fawn to be considered distinctly objectionable and not to be encouraged.

Size—Twenty-two inches and upwards for dogs and slightly less for bitches. Type, character and symmetry are of the greatest importance and are on no account to be sacrificed to size alone.

General Appearance and Characteristics—A strong, compact-looking dog of great symmetry, practically the same in measurement from shoulder to stern as in height, absolutely free from legginess or weasleness, very elastic in his gallop, but in walking or trotting he has a characteristic ambling or pacing movement, and his bark should be loud, with a peculiar "pot-casse" ring in it. Taking him all round, he is profusely, but not excessively coated, thick-set, muscular, able-bodied dog with a most intelligent expression, free from all Poodle or Deerhound character. Soundness should be considered of greatest importance.

SCALE OF POINTS

Skull	5	Body and Loins	10
Eyes	5	Hindquarters	10
Ears	5	Legs	10
Teeth	5	Coat (Texture, Quality and	
Nose	5	Condition)	15
Jaw	5	General Appearance and	
Foreface	5	Movement	15
Neck and Shoulders	5	Total	100

2. Breed Requirements

EXERCISE NEEDED

The average Old English Sheepdog is a peppy, playful creature, bounding with enthusiastic energy when running free and at play. He is particularly agile and picturesque when seen galloping over the turf.

The average adult house pet should be allowed to run vigorously twice a day morning and evening. These romps should become standard practice as part of the daily care pattern and should be scheduled for the same time each day. In addition to the free play period your dog should be walked at a steady pace of at least one mile a day. A dog confined as a house pet should be allowed to relieve himself every three to four hours during the day time. Kennel or yard dogs usually will take enough active exercise on their own to maintain fitness provided the area enclosing them is spacious.

Puppies should be restricted from over stimulating experiences and over-

A litter of three-week-old puppies. The Old English Sheepdog must have the very best in care and feeding if he is to attain his full size and the majestic coat that is the hallmark and heritage of the breed.

active play for extended periods of time. Treat your pup as if it were a toddler. Remembering that young toddlers play actively for short periods of time and require good food, fresh air, sunlight and much rest.

PLAYTHINGS

Toys for your puppy or adult dog make him more interesting and the results of dogs raised with and without toys parallel the recorded results of deprived, underprivileged youngsters as compared to those having received an enriched background. Make certain that the toys you select are not easily chewed. Rubber balls and rubber bones must be of the toughest sort. Beef knuckle and shin bones with all traces of meat removed are ideal when cut to 6 inch lengths. They are just about indestructible. But preferable to these are the artificial bones made of nylon (Nylabone). These have been shown to be the safest of all chewing articles.

FOOD REQUIREMENTS FOR THE ADULT

You may have often heard the statement "We are what we eat." This holds equally true for your dog. We have always maintained that in the formula applied in raising and maintaining good dogs, that "half is breeding and half is feeding." The average adult Old English Sheepdog should be fed once a day. Late afternoon feeding is most desirable.

The diet should consist of a good commercial brand kibble or meal to provide proper bulk and carbohydrates and clean, fresh meat (beef is recommended as the basic source of protein). Liver, fowl, and lamb as well as cottage cheese, and eggs enhance the diet and provide additional vitamins and food value. These foods alone are not sufficient however and additional vitamins must be fed and included in the diet in the form of tablets or powders. Vitamin A, D and calcium are extremely important.

The adult Bob-tail will eat one and a half to three pounds of food a day depending upon his environment. If your dog is to be your house pet one pound of meat and 2 to 3 cups of kibble or meal will nourish him well. If your dog is kept out doors in unheated quarters and an active worker with a flock of sheep or cattle he will require at least 2 pounds of meat and perhaps up to 4 or 5 cups of kibble or meal daily as a minimum diet.

COLLARS AND LEADS

The use of proper collars is especially important for your dog. The neck coat is easily cut, discolored and broken and the recommended collar is made of rolled (round) leather $\frac{1}{2}$ inch in diameter and averaging from 19 inches to 24 inches in full circumference when buckled around the throat of the dog. Naturally a small animal will use a 19 inch collar and a larger more heavily coated specimen will require a larger size. Make certain if the collar is other than a natural color it will not bleed into the coat of the dog when the coat is wet.

Chain choke collars are not recommended because of their tearing action and when left upon the dog for any prolonged period of time they will oxidize and discolor the coat. If a choke collar is required as a last resort measure for an unruly animal make certain that it is not left on the dog in between walks or training sessions. Rolled leather choke collars may be purchased quite readily and afford added control for the dog learning to heel.

Harnesses should never be used especially in the case of young puppies. They confine proper shoulder action and gait, and cut coat.

Leads should be of a strong grade of rawhide or saddle leather. They should attach to the collar with a dependable snap or spring action fastener. The lead may be of either rolled or flat cut leather $\frac{1}{2}$ inch to 1 inch in diameter and should be at least 4 feet in length. Chain leads tangle in the coat, usually rust from damp and wet weather, wear out gloves and tend to cut the hands of the person holding or walking the dog. Their use is not advised. Young puppies may be lead broken with a lightweight flat "cat" collar. The lighter the weight the better. A lightweight lead is also suggested for this training. A heavy, clumsy lead used for the initial lead breaking sessions often frightens and hampers the uninitiated youngster.

HOUSING AND SHELTER

Your puppy or adult dog will be best adjusted leading his complete life span housed with you. I have never known one of the breed who did not prefer to be with the family and its master. The Old English Sheepdog is equally at home in an apartment or house. They thrive on human companionship and although they adjust to kennel life they prefer company.

If you must confine your dog in a kennel or pen make sure to provide proper shade, shelter from wind and rain and an easily available supply of fresh water.

The area where your dog is housed and sleeps should be draft free, warm and dry. Your dog should not be allowed to sleep on concrete or stone for long periods of time. You may note when kept as a house dog your pride and joy may seek out the bathroom or linoleum kitchen floor as his favorite resting place. Often the static electricity of rugs and carpeting (especially nylon) will create an allergy or tend to make your dog scratch.

Small kennel type dog houses are not recommended but if an absolute necessity make certain it is large enough to allow your dog to turn about easily within its confines and that it is raised above ground level for insulation and to allow for drainage from collected water or dampness. It is essential that there be proper air space under the roof as well.

GEOGRAPHIC AND CLIMATIC LIMITATIONS

The breed adapts to all climates. I have never known of one in the 32 years of association and experience with the breed that met with any difficulties because of climatic or geographic conditions. In the tropics the undercoat

Ch. Beckington Lady of Welby House, owned and handled by Mrs. Mabel Gibson. Sire: Shepton Bridewell Brave Brigadier; dam: Shepton Butterfly. This bitch is the record holding Challenge Certificate winner in Great Britain with a total of 28 C.C.'s. She is shown winning best in show at the Blackpool Canine Society under judge Wilson Wyle.

will not grow as dense and the dog may require more frequent grooming to keep mats from forming. In cold climates nature provides a thicker growth of undercoat which acts as insulation against snow, rain and sleet.

It is important to remember that almost any location geographically has its own variety of burrs, foxtails or thistles. It is very important to check your dog regularly for these aggravating and bothersome seeds of vegetation. Often they are easily overlooked and work their way down into the coat and into the skin causing infections and skin abrasions. I have known a small grass seed to be so irritating as to make a dog tear and chew away at his coat and skin in a futile attempt to relieve himself of foreign matter. A watchful eye is a helpful asset when one is alerted to these possible dangers.

3. Grooming

To maintain the typical coat so highly prized by the pet and show dog owner proper and regular grooming sessions are essential.

FREQUENCY OF GROOMING

Grooming should be done in a quiet place either on the floor or on a suitable, sturdy table of adequate size for the dog in question. The adult Old English Sheepdog should be groomed regularly once a week. Puppies may be groomed more frequently so as to become more acquainted with grooming implements and procedures. It is debatable as to which is more harmful, negligence or over-zealous, heavy-handed grooming techniques. Either culprit can ruin the natural bloom of the coat. Overgroom and you loose undercoat and guard hairs. Omit a weekly grooming session and the coat will begin to mat requiring much additional grooming time and loss of coat.

GROOMING MATERIALS

A steel comb about 4 inches in length with round teeth set about $\frac{3}{8}$ of an inch apart and of about 3 inches in length is an important part of your equipment. The comb may be used as a pick to comb out dead coat but should never be used indiscriminately with a heavy hand.

There are several types of useful brushes. Each serves a valuable and specific function. The rubber padded slicker, or Poodle brush, with short slanting metal pins is best used to fluff up leg, chest or head coat. It should never be used routinely over the entire dog. A brush of whalebone, rice root or one which is rubber cushioned with flexible stainless steel pins are splendid for general brushing. The latter outlives the other two previously mentioned for length of service. The one I write of is an imported item from England.

A good quality straight blade barbers scissors will also be important for the rounding of the coat at the dog's feet. If the coat is left to its normal growth around the toes and feet the illusion is that of being down at the pasterns and as though he is wearing snow shoes. It is also the best implement to use for scissoring and clearing the area near the base of the spine and tail for sanitary reasons. A small $3\frac{1}{2}$ inch infant's nail cutting scissors with rounded tips is ideal for removing the excess wadded hair which accumulates so prolifically between the toes.

God's gift of a good pair of hands and strong fingers are of added benefit.

The hands do the best job of opening and breaking up clustered mats. Additional aids to expedite grooming are a mat splitter; also the end point of the comb may be employed for this usage. The mat splitter will work more quickly but will also take much more coat off the dog.

The comb should be used sparingly but should always be used in the direction of the normal lay and growth of the hair. The comb is of special benefit used on the areas behind the ears, around the mouth, near the eyes, between the forelegs, the elbows and the scrotal area of the male and vulva parts of the bitch. For convenience, brushing and combing are more easily done with the dog lying on its side. The last touch up brushing is done with the dog standing on all fours. The coat on the head is always brushed in a forward and downward direction as is the coat of the neck and shoulders. All the other body areas including the legs and chest are brushed up against the natural lay of the hair. The coat on the back should be brushed forward.

Grooming of puppies is best begun at the age of 4 or 5 weeks of age. Care

Ch. Shayloran's Billy Hayseed, owned and handled by the Author and bred by Mr. and Mrs. Harold F. Richards. Sire: Beckington Reprint; dam: Rosmoore Pink Lady. This upstanding male has a record as a producer to equal his successes in the show ring. He is shown winning the working group at the San Luis Obispo Kennel Club under judge Vincent Perry.

should be taken to make certain that the eyes and mouth are kept clean. Food and eye matter tend to cake up in the coat. Fecal matter may cake without being easily visible in the tail area, so early scissoring of puppies is important. The best implement for young puppy grooming is a metal handled comb with a 4 inch head. The over-all length is about 7 inches. The teeth of this comb should be round and blunt at the tips and spaced about $\frac{1}{4}$ of an inch apart. Brushing is not generally begun until the puppy is 7 weeks of age. Claw trimming is an important part of the grooming session. Puppies should have their claws trimmed or cut with the small child's blunt nosed scissors no later than the fourth day after birth. They should be checked regularly at weekly intervals until 2 months of age. At that time a regular canine-type claw clipper may be used. Claws of the adolescent puppy and grown dog should be checked on a bi-weekly schedule. It should become a routine pedicure process which also includes the removal of hair between the pads of the feet.

The average puppy starts developing its longer and heavier more mature guard hairs at about seven to eight months of age. It is at this stage of develop-

Ch. Shaggybar Bottomsup, owned and bred by Mr. Stan Goldberg. Sire: Ch. Woodruff; dam: Greyfriar Angel Feathers. This handsome dog was just over four years old at the time of his death and had already won two bests in show. He is shown winning the breed at the Santa Ana Valley Kennel Club under judge Rutledge Gilliland. His passing is a great loss to the breed.

ment that the coat requires some additional care. Actually this change of coat period may well last until the dog is 14 months of age. The heavy guard hair growth is held back by the dense soft puppy coat and frequently mats close to the skin. The wiry textured guard hairs being held down close to the skin by the weight of the mat formations irritate the skin and tend to make the young dog scratch and tear at himself.

TECHNIQUE FOR MAT REMOVAL

After locating the matted area, concentrate on a two inch square section. Using the thumbs and index fingers of both hands gently pull and break the mat apart. Always pull in an outward horizontal direction to either side. Never exert pull or pressure in a direct line from the skin. When the mat has been softened and partially broken apart the comb may be used to remove the dead and broken coat. Having cleared the mats in this manner the pin or whale bone brush may be used to brush through the free hair. When a mat is so tenacious that the fingers cannot make sufficient headway the end teeth of the large toothed comb may be used in a picking action. Care must be taken to hold the matted hair firmly with the left hand so that the pull exerted by the comb does not pain the dog. If the comb does not do the job the mat splitter may be used to cut through the mat in a vertical direction pulling away from the dog's skin.

The ears should be regularly checked for excessive inner ear hair growth. There are many suggested techniques of hair pulling and clearing of the inner ear including chemicals and swabs. None of these practices will be recommended here. The external under ear flap may be cleansed with a soft piece of toweling dampened with warm water. Hair pulling or cleansing of the inner ear should be done by your veterinarian.

BATHING

It is not recommended that the Old English Sheepdog be bathed as a general practice. It softens the coat, removes the natural oils of the coat and increases the possibility of matting. Puppies should never be bathed before the age of six months. Sometimes a bath becomes a necessity due to the infestation of vermin and parasites, which because of the breed's dense coat cannot be too easily removed by the usual use of flea powders and sprays. May we suggest at this point that "An ounce of prevention is worth a pound of cure." It has been a most successful practice to dust and spray dogs of the breed routinely, especially during the hot weather months thus avoiding any possible problems caused by lice, ticks, and fleas.

Should a bath be required for reasons of health or unusual circumstances you will find the following equipment helpful. A quart metal or plastic container (preferably one with a handle) for applying a good quality canine shampoo. Human products tend to remove oils from the coat and may also irritate the skin. Bathing equipment includes a hose type spray or quart pan for adequate rinsing, a bottle or block of laundry blueing to be used in the rinse water, a dozen thirsty bath towels, and last, but not least, a standard bath tub.

The tub should be half filled with tepid water. Then lift the dog into the tub. Calm and reassure him that all is well. Slowly saturate the entire dog with water. Proceed to apply shampoo or parasite medication as your requirements demand. Gently work up a lather. Avoid letting the shampoo run into the dog's eyes, mouth or nostrils. Using either hose spray or pan, rinse very thoroughly with fresh, warm, clear water. Empty the tub with the dog still in it. This method allows the dog to drip and drain freely while still in the tub avoiding a major flood of water on the bathroom or grooming room floor. Squeeze sections of coat over the entire dog and lift each leg in turn wringing the water from the coat. Remove the dog from the tub and allow him a moment or two to shake himself free of additional excess moisture. Next freely start using bath towels or toweling and work away until the dog is

Ch. Momarv's Mighty Like a Rose, owned and bred by the Author. Sire: Ch. Shayloran's Billy Hayseed; dam: Momarv's Burning Bright. This handsome youngster, line-bred on the immortal Ch. Merriedip Duke, has already proven to be a worthy winner.

completely dry. Areas under the chest and between the forelegs are apt to remain damp. Double check these spots. The comb or brush should never be used when the dog is wet or damp. When completely dry the dog should be allowed a short romp to relieve himself and a thorough brushing should follow.

DRY BATH METHOD

This is the method usually employed as a general practice for cleaning and whitening your pet or show dog for sanitary reasons and general appearance sake. In addition to the basic grooming tools previously mentioned secure a small metal $\frac{1}{2}$ quart dish, (1) 4 inch by 6 inch synthetic sponge, 1 box corn starch, powdered chalk or bolted whiting.

Stand the dog on a grooming table, floor (well covered with newspapers) or out of doors on the grass. Fill $\frac{1}{2}$ quart container $\frac{3}{4}$ with water and add a small amount of shampoo (just enough to make a rich suds solution). Take your sponge and submerge into shampoo solution and wring almost completely dry. With sponge in hand moisten beard and mouth area with suds. Then quickly towel dry. Repeat this process tackling each of the four legs and feet, chest, head, neck and abdominal areas where dust and grime accumulate but are not easily visible. All white areas should be so sponged and you may continue to the rear portion of the dog's body marked in blue as well.

The suds sponging system removes all surface dirt. If a disinfectant is desired it may be included in the suds water. Be sure to use only strengths directed remembering that the quantity of water you are working with is small. After toweling all the suds off these areas the dog's coat will be surface damp. Take corn starch, chalk or whiting and lightly (ever so lightly) dust

Ch. Shepton Surprise, owned by the Author and bred by Miss C. M. Steer. Sire: Nicefella of Danehurst; dam: Shepton Perfect Surprise. This English imported bitch was a best in show dog as well as the winner of many groups.

on to the surface coat of the white marked areas. Pat briskly so as to remove all visible excess of cleaner. Now take up your pin brush or whale bone brush and apply the good over-all brushing your dog will enjoy. No portion of the dog should be left unbrushed. Make certain that all traces of chalk, corn starch or powdered cleaner are completely removed, and with a damp cloth, wipe off nose and pads of the feet. Make certain that the eyes are cleaned and wiped free from any collected matter.

Your dog should now be a dazzling picture ready to compete in the show ring or to grace your family circle in all his radiant splendor.

4. The New Puppy

PREPARING FOR THE PUPPY'S ARRIVAL

Because at least three out of four prospective purchasers of dogs want to buy a young rather than an adult or almost adult dog, the problem of preparing for the arrival of a permanent canine house guest almost always means preparing for the arrival of a puppy. This is not to say that there is anything wrong with purchasing an adult dog; on the contrary, such a purchase has definite advantages in that it often allows freedom from housebreaking chores and rigorous feeding schedules, and these are of definite benefit to prospective purchasers who have little time to spare. Since the great majority of dog buyers, however, prefer to watch their pet grow from sprawlingly playful puppyhood to dignified maturity, buying a dog, practically speaking, means buying a puppy.

Before you get a puppy be sure that you are willing to take the responsibility of training him and caring for his physical needs. His early training is most important, as an adult dog that is a well-behaved member of the family is the end product of your early training. Remember that your new puppy knows only a life of romping with his littermates and the security of being with his mother, and that coming into your home is a new and sometimes frightening experience for him. He will adjust quickly if you are patient with him and show him what you expect of him. If there are small children in the family be sure that they do not abuse him or play roughly with him. A puppy plays hard, but he also requires frequent periods of rest. Before he comes, decide where he is to sleep and where he is to eat. If your puppy does not have a collar, find out the size he requires and buy an inexpensive one, as he will soon outgrow it. Have the proper grooming equipment on hand. Consult the person from whom you bought the puppy as to the proper food for your puppy, and learn the feeding time and amount that he eats a day. Buy him some toys—usually the breeder will give you some particular toy or toys which he has cherished as a puppy to add to his new ones and to make him less homesick. Get everything you need from your petshop *before* you bring the puppy home.

MALE OR FEMALE?

Before buying your puppy you should have made a decision as to whether you want a male or a female. Unless you want to breed your pet and raise a litter of puppies, your preference as to the sex of your puppy is strictly a personal choice. Both sexes are pretty much the same in disposition and character, and both make equally good pets.

WHERE TO BUY YOUR PUPPY

Although petshop owners are necessarily restricted from carrying all breeds in stock, they know the best dog breeders and are sometimes able to supply quality puppies on demand. In cases in which a petshop owner is unable to obtain a dog for you, he can still refer you to a good source, such as a reputable kennel. If your local petshop proprietor is unable to either obtain a dog for you or refer you to someone from whom you can purchase one, don't give up: there are other avenues to explore. The American Kennel Club will furnish you addresses. Additional sources of information are the various magazines devoted to the dog fancy.

SIGNS OF GOOD HEALTH

Picking out a healthy, attractive little fellow to join the family circle is a different matter from picking a show dog; it is also a great deal less complicated. Often the puppy will pick you. If he does, and it is mutual admiration at first sight, he is the best puppy for you. At a reliable kennel or petshop the owner will be glad to answer your questions and to point out the difference between pet and show-quality puppies. Trust your eyes and hands to tell if the puppies are sound in body and temperament. Ears and eyes should not have suspicious discharges. Legs should have strong bones; bodies should have solid muscles. Coats should be clean. Lift the hair to see if the skin is free of scales and parasites.

Temperament can vary from puppy to puppy in the same litter. There is always one puppy which will impress you by his energy and personality. He loves to show off and will fling himself all over you and his littermates, and everyone who comes to see the puppies falls in love with him. However, do not overlook the more reserved puppy. Most dogs are wary of strangers, so reserve may indicate caution, not a timid puppy. He may calmly accept your presence when he senses that all is well. Such a puppy should be a steady reliable dog when mature. In any event, never force yourself on a puppy — let him come to you. Reliable breeders and petshops will urge you to take your puppy to the veterinarian of your choice to have the puppy's health checked, and will allow you at least two days in which to have it done. It should be clearly understood whether rejection by a veterinarian for health reasons means that you have the choice of another puppy from that litter or that you get your money back.

AGE AT WHICH PUPPY SHOULD BE PURCHASED

A puppy should be at least six weeks of age before you take him home. Many breeders will not let puppies go before they are two months old. In general, the puppy you buy for show and breeding should be five or six months old. If you want a show dog, remember that not even an expert can predict with 100% accuracy what a small puppy will be when he grows up

PAPERS

When you buy a purebred dog you should receive his American Kennel Club registration certificate (or an application form to fill out), a pedigree, and a health certificate made out by the breeder's veterinarian. The registration certificate is the official A.K.C. paper. If the puppy was named and registered by his breeder you will want to complete the transfer and send it, with the fee, to the American Kennel Club. They will transfer the dog to your ownership in their records and send a new certificate to you. If you receive, instead, an application for registration, you should fill it out, choosing a name for your dog, and mail it, with the fee, to the A.K.C.

The pedigree is a chart showing your puppy's ancestry and is not a part of his official papers. The health certificate will tell what shots have been given and when the next ones are due. Your veterinarian will be appreciative of this information, and will continue with the same series of shots if they have not been completed. The health certificate will also give the dates on which the puppy has been wormed. Ask your veterinarian whether rabies shots are required in your locality. Most breeders will give you food for a few days along with instructions for feeding so that your puppy will have the same diet he is accustomed to until you can buy a supply at your petshop.

THE PUPPY'S FIRST NIGHT WITH YOU

The puppy's first night at home is likely to be disturbing to the family. Keep in mind that suddenly being away from his mother, brothers, and sisters is a new experience for him; he may be confused and frightened. If you have a special room in which you have his bed, be sure that there is nothing there with which he can harm himself. Be sure that all lamp cords are out of his reach and that there is nothing that he can tip or pull over. Check furniture that he might get stuck under or behind and objects that he might chew. If you want him to sleep in your room he probably will be quiet all night, reassured by your presence. If left in a room by himself he will cry and howl, and you will have to steel yourself to be impervious to his whining. After a few nights alone he will adjust. The first night that he is alone it is wise to put a loud-ticking alarm clock, as well as his toys, in the room with him. The alarm clock will make a comforting noise, and he will not feel that he is alone.

YOUR PUPPY'S BED

Every dog likes to have a place that is his alone. He holds nothing more sacred than his own bed whether it be a rug, dog crate, or dog bed. If you get your puppy a bed be sure to get one which discourages chewing. Also be sure that the bed is large enough to be comfortable for him when he is fully grown. Locate it away from drafts and radiators. A word might be said here in defense of the crate, which many pet owners think is cruel and confining. Given a choice, a young dog instinctively selects a secure place

Special dog feeding and watering utensils are so designed as to safeguard your pet from dangerous porcelain chips. These utensils are easy to keep clean, too.

in which to lounge, rest, or sleep. The walls and ceiling of a crate, even a wire one, answer that need. Once he regards his crate as a safe and reassuring place to stay, you will be able to leave him alone in the house.

FEEDING YOUR PUPPY

As a general rule, a puppy from weaning time (six weeks) to three months of age should have *four meals a day;* from three months to six months, *three meals;* from six months to one year, *two meals.* After a year, a dog does well on *one meal daily.* There are as many feeding schedules as there are breeders, and puppies do fine on all of them, so it is best for the new owner to follow the one given him by the breeder of his puppy. Remember that all dogs are individuals. The amount that will keep your dog in good health is right for him, not the "rule-book" amount. A feeding schedule to give you some idea of what the average puppy will eat is as follows:

Morning meal: Puppy meal with milk.

Afternoon meal: Meat mixed with puppy meal, plus a vitamin-mineral supplement.

Evening meal: Same as afternoon meal, but without a vitamin-mineral supplement.

Do not change the amounts in your puppy's diet too rapidly. If he gets diarrhea it may be that he is eating too much, so cut back on his food and when he is normal again increase his food more slowly.

There is a canned food made especially for puppies which you can buy only by a veterinarian's prescription. Some breeders use this very successfully from weaning to three months.

TRANSITIONAL DIET

Changing over to an adult program of feeding is not difficult. Very often the puppy will change himself; that is, he will refuse to eat some of his meals. He adjusts to his one meal (or two meals) a day without any trouble at all.

BREAKING TO COLLAR AND LEASH

Puppies are usually broken to a collar before you bring them home, but even if yours has never worn one it is a simple matter to get him used to it. Put a loose collar on him for a few hours at a time. At first he may scratch at it and try to get it off, but gradually he will take it as a matter of course. To break him to a lead, attach his leash to his collar and let him drag it around. When he becomes used to it pick it up and gently pull him in the direction you want him to go. He will think it is a game, and with a bit of patience on your part he will allow himself to be led.

DISCIPLINING YOUR PUPPY

The way to have a well-mannered adult dog is to give him firm basic training while he is a puppy. When you say "No" you must mean "No." Your dog will respect you only if you are firm. A six- to eight-weeks-old puppy is old enough to understand what "No" means. The first time you see your puppy doing something he shouldn't be doing, chewing something he shouldn't chew, or wandering in a forbidden area, it's time to teach him. Shout, "No." Puppies do not like loud noises, and your misbehaving pet will readily connect the word with something unpleasant. Usually a firm "No" in a disapproving tone of voice is enough to correct your dog, but occasionally you get a puppy that requires a firmer hand, especially as he grows older. In this case hold your puppy firmly and slap him gently across the hindquarters. If this seems cruel, you should realize that no dog resents being disciplined if he is caught in the act of doing something wrong, and your puppy will be intelligent enough to know what the slap was for.

After you have slapped him and you can see that he has learned his lesson, call him to you and talk to him in a pleasant tone of voice — praise him for coming to you. This sounds contradictory, but it works with a puppy. He immediately forgives you, practically tells you that it was his fault and that he deserved his punishment, and promises that it will not happen again. This form of discipline works best and may be used for all misbehaviors.

Never punish your puppy by chasing him around, making occasional swipes with a rolled-up newspaper; punish him only when you have a firm hold on him. Above all, never punish your dog after having called him to you. He must learn to associate coming to you with something pleasant.

HOUSEBREAKING

While housebreaking your puppy do not let him have the run of the house. If you do you will find that he will pick out his own bathroom, which may be in your bedroom or in the middle of the living room rug. Keep him confined to a small area where you can watch him, and you will be able to train him much more easily and speedily. A puppy does not want to dirty his bed, but he does need to be taught where he should go. Spread papers over his living quarters, then watch him carefully. When you notice him starting to whimper, sniff the floor, or run agitatedly in little circles, rush him to the place that you want to serve as his relief area and gently hold him there until he relieves himself. Then praise him lavishly. When you remove the soiled papers, leave a small damp piece so that the puppy's sense of smell will lead him back there next time. If he makes a mistake, wash the area at once with warm water, followed by a rinse with water and vinegar or sudsy ammonia. This will kill the odor and prevent discoloration. It shouldn't take more than a few days for him to get the idea of using newspapers. When he becomes fairly consistent, reduce the area of paper to a few sheets in a corner. As soon as you think he has the idea fixed in his mind, you can let him roam around the house a bit, but keep an eye on him. It might be best to keep him on leash the first few days so that you can rush him back to his paper at any signs of an approaching accident.

The normal healthy puppy will want to relieve himself when he wakes up in the morning, after each feeding, and after strenuous exercise. During early puppyhood any excitement, such as the return home of a member of the family or the approach of a visitor, may result in floor-wetting, but that phase should pass in a few weeks. Keep in mind that you can't expect too much from your puppy until he is about five months old. Before that, his muscles and digestive system just aren't under his control.

OUTDOOR HOUSEBREAKING

You can begin outdoor training on leash even while you are paper-training your puppy. First thing in the morning take him outdoors (to the curb, if you are in the city) and walk him back and forth in a small area until he relieves himself. He will probably make a puddle and then walk around, uncertain of what is expected of him. You can try standing him over a newspaper, which may give him the idea. Some dog trainers use glycerine suppositories at this point for fast action. Praise your dog every time taking him outside brings results, and he will get the idea. You'll find, when you begin the outdoor training, that the male puppy usually requires a longer walk than the female. Both male and female puppies will squat. It isn't until he is older that the male dog will begin to lift his leg. If you hate to give up your sleep, you can train your puppy to go outdoors during the day and use the paper at night.

5. Training

WHEN TO START TRAINING

You should never begin SERIOUS obedience training before your dog is seven or eight months old. (Some animal psychologists state that puppies can begin training when seven weeks old, if certain techniques are followed. These techniques, however, are still experimental and should be left to the professional trainer to prove their worth.) While your dog is still in his early puppyhood, concentrate on winning his confidence so he will love and admire you. This will make his training easier, since he will do anything to please you. Basic training can be started at the age of three or four months. He should be taught to walk nicely on a leash, sit and lie down on command, and come when he is called.

YOUR PART IN TRAINING

You must patiently demonstrate to your dog what each word of command means. Guide him with your hands and the training leash, reassuring him with your voice, through whatever routine you are teaching him. Repeat the word associated with the act. Demonstrate again and again to give the dog a chance to make the connection in his mind.

Once he begins to get the idea, use the word of command without any physical guidance. Drill him. When he makes mistakes, correct him, kindly at first, more severely as his training progresses. Try not to lose your patience or become irritated, and never slap him with your hand or the leash during the training session. Withholding praise or rebuking him will make him feel bad enough.

When he does what you want, praise him lavishly with words and with pats. Don't continually reward with dog candy or treats in training. The dog that gets into the habit of performing for a treat will seldom be fully dependable when he can't smell or see one in the offing. When he carries out a command, even though his performance is slow or sloppy, praise him and he will perform more readily the next time.

THE TRAINING VOICE

When you start training your dog, use your training voice, giving commands in a firm, clear tone. Once you give a command, persist until it is obeyed, even if you have to pull the dog to obey you. He must learn that training is different from playing, that a command once given must be obeyed no matter what distractions are present. Remember that the tone and pitch of your voice, not loudness, are the qualities that will influence your dog most.

Be consistent in the use of words during training. Confine your commands to as few words as possible and never change them. It is best for only one person to carry on the dog's training, because different people will use different words and tactics that will confuse your dog. The dog who hears *"come," "get over here," "hurry up," "here, Rex,"* and other commands when he is wanted will become totally confused.

TRAINING LESSONS

Training is hard on the dog — and on the trainer. A young dog just cannot take more than ten minutes of training at a stretch, so limit the length of your first lessons. Then you can gradually increase the length of time to about thirty minutes. You'll find that you too will tend to become impatient when you stretch out a training lesson. If you find yourself losing your temper, stop and resume the lesson at another time. Before and after each lesson have a play period, but don't play during a training session. Even the youngest dog soon learns that schooling is a serious matter; fun comes afterward.

Don't spend too much time on one phase of the training, or the dog will become bored. Always try to end a lesson on a pleasant note. Actually, in nine cases out of ten, if your dog isn't doing what you want it's because you're not getting the idea over to him properly.

YOUR TRAINING EQUIPMENT AND ITS USE

The leash is more properly called the lead, so we'll use that term here. The best leads for training are the six-foot webbed-cloth leads, usually olive-drab in color, and the six-foot leather lead. Fancier leads are available and may be used if desired.

You'll need a metal-link collar, called a choke chain, consisting of a metal chain with rings on each end. Even though the name may sound frightening, it won't hurt your dog, and it is an absolute MUST in training. There is a right and a wrong way to put the training collar on. It should go around the dog's neck so that you can attach the lead to the ring at the end of the chain which passes OVER, not under his neck. It is most important that the collar is put on properly so it will tighten when the lead is pulled and ease when you relax your grip.

The correct way to hold the lead is also very important, as the collar should have some slack in it, at all times, except when correcting. Holding the loop in your right hand, extend your arm out to the side, even with your shoulder. With your left hand, grasp the lead as close as possible to the collar, without making it tight. The remaining portion of the lead can be made into a loop which is held in the right hand. Keep this arm close to your body. Most corrections will be made with the left hand by giving the lead a jerk in the direction you want the dog to go. The dog that pulls and forges ahead can be corrected by a steady pull on the lead.

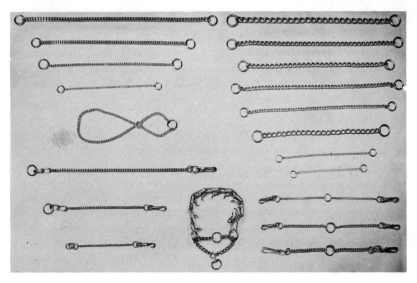

Special training collars for your dog can be purchased at your petshop.

HEELING

"*Heeling*" in dog language means having your dog walk alongside you on your left side, close to your leg, on lead or off. With patience and effort you can train your dog to walk with you even on a crowded street or in the presence of other dogs.

Now that you have learned the correct way to put on your dog's collar and how to hold the lead, you are ready to start with his first lesson in heeling. Put the dog at your left side, sitting. Using the dog's name and the command "*Heel*," start forward on your LEFT foot, giving a tug on the lead to get the dog started. Always use the dog's name first, followed by the command, such as "*Rex, heel*." Saying his name will help get his attention and will let him know that you are about to give a command.

Walk briskly, with even steps, going around in a large circle, square, or straight line. While walking, make sure that your dog stays on the left side and close to your leg. If he lags behind, give several tugs on the lead to get him up to you, then praise him for doing well. If he forges ahead or swings wide, stop and jerk the lead sharply and bring him back to the proper position. Always repeat the command when correcting, and praise him when he does well. If your dog continues to pull or lag behind, either your corrections are not severe enough or your timing between correction and praise is off. Do this exercise for only five minutes at first, gradually lengthening it to fifteen, or even half an hour.

To keep your dog's attention, talk to him as you keep him in place. You can also do a series of fast about-turns, giving the lead a jerk as you turn. He will gradually learn that he must pay attention or be jerked to your side. You can vary the routine by changing speeds, doing turns, figure-eights, and by zig-zagging across the training area.

"HEEL" MEANS "SIT," TOO

To the dog, the command "*Heel*" will also mean that he has to sit in the heel position at your left side when you stop walking — with no additional command from you. As you practice heeling, make him sit whenever you stop, at first using the word "*Sit*," then with no command at all. He'll soon get the idea and sit down when you stop and wait for the command "*Heel*" to start walking again.

TRAINING TO SIT

Training your dog to sit should be fairly easy. Stand him on your left side, holding the lead fairly short, and command him to "*Sit*." As you give the verbal command, pull up slightly with the lead and push his hindquarters down. Do not let him lie down or stand up. Keep him in a sitting position for a moment, then release the pressure on the lead and praise him. Constantly repeat the command as you hold him in a sitting position, thus fitting the word to the action in his mind. After a while he will begin to get the idea and will sit without your having to push his hindquarters down. When he reaches that stage, insist that he sit on command. If he is slow to obey, slap his hindquarters with your hand to get him down fast. *DO NOT HIT HIM HARD!* Teach him to sit on command facing you as well as when he is at your side. When he begins sitting on command with the lead on, try it with the lead off.

THE "LIE DOWN"

The object of this is to get the dog to lie down either on the verbal command "*Down*" or when you give him the hand signal, your hand raised in front of you, palm down. This is one of the most important parts of training. A well-trained dog will drop on command and stay down whatever the temptation: cat-chasing, car-chasing, or another dog across the street.

Don't start training to lie down until the dog is almost letter-perfect in sitting on command. Then place the dog in a sit, and kneel before him. With both hands, reach forward to his legs and take one front leg in each hand, thumbs up, and holding just below his elbows. Lift his legs slightly off the ground and pull them somewhat out in front of him. Simultaneously, give the command "*Down*" and lower his front legs to the ground.

Hold the dog down and stroke him to let him know that staying down is what you want him to do. This method is far better than forcing a young dog down. Using force can cause him to become very frightened and he will begin to dislike any training. Always talk to your dog and let him know that you are very pleased with him, and soon you will find that you have a happy working dog.

After he begins to get the idea, slide the lead under your left foot and give the command "*Down.*" At the same time, pull the lead. This will help get the dog down. Meanwhile, raise your hand in the down signal. Don't expect to accomplish all this in one session. Be patient and work with the dog. He'll cooperate if you show him just what you expect him to do.

THE "STAY"

The next step is to train your dog to stay either in a "*Sit*" or "*Down*" position. Sit him at your side. Give the command "*Stay,*" but be careful not to use his name with this command, because hearing his name may lead him to think that some action is expected of him. If he begins to move, repeat "*Stay*" firmly and hold him down in the sit. Constantly repeat the word "*Stay*" to fix the meaning of that command in his mind. After he has learned to stay for a short time, gradually increase the length of his stay. The hand signal for the stay is a downward sweep of your hand toward the dog's nose, with the palm facing him. While he is sitting, walk around him and stand in front of him. Hold the lead at first; later, drop the lead on the ground in front of him and keep him sitting. If he bolts, scold him and place him back in the same position, repeating the command and all the exercise.

Use some word such as "*Okay*" or "*Up*" to let him know when he can get up, and praise him well for a good performance. As this practice continues, walk farther and farther away from him. Later, try sitting him, giving the command to stay, and then walk out of sight, first for a few seconds, then for longer periods. A well-trained dog should stay where you put him without moving until you come and release him.

Similarly, practice having him stay in the down position, first with you near him, later when you step out of sight.

THE "COME" ON COMMAND

You can train your dog to come when you call him, if you begin when he is young. At first, work with him on lead. Sit the dog, then back away the length of the lead and call him, putting into your voice as much coaxing affection as possible. Give an easy tug on the lead to get him started. When he does come, make a big fuss over him; it might help at this point to give him a small piece of dog candy or food as a reward. He should get the idea soon. You can also move away from him the full length of the lead and call to him something like "*Rex, come,*" then run backward a few steps and stop, making him sit directly in front of you.

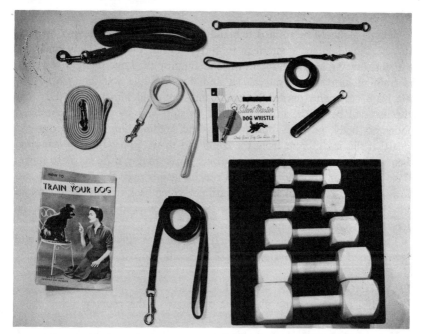

Visit your petshop for all of the training equipment you will need to make your pet a better canine citizen.

Don't be too eager to practice coming on command off lead. Wait until you are certain that you have the dog under perfect control before you try calling him when he's free. Once he gets the idea that he can disobey a command and get away with it, your training program will suffer a serious setback. Keep in mind that your dog's life may depend on his immediate response to a command to come when he is called. If he disobeys off lead, put the lead back on and correct him severely with jerks of the lead.

TEACHING TO COME TO HEEL

The object of this is for you to stand still, say "*Heel*," and have your dog come right over to you and sit by your left knee in the heel position. If your dog has been trained to sit without command every time you stop, he's ready for this step.

Sit him in front of and facing you and step back one step. Moving only your left foot, pull the dog behind you, then step forward and pull him around until he is in a heel position. You can also have the dog go around by passing the lead behind your back. Use your left heel to straighten him out if he begins to sit behind you or crookedly. This may take a little work, but he will get the idea if you show him just what you want.

THE "STAND"

Your dog should be trained to stand in one spot without moving his feet, and he should allow a stranger to run his hand over his body and legs without showing any resentment or fear. Employ the same method you used in training him to stay on the sit and down. While walking, place your left hand out, palm toward his nose, and command him to stay. His first impulse will be to sit, so be prepared to stop him by placing your hand under his body, near his hindquarters, and holding him until he gets the idea that this is different from the command to sit. Praise him for standing, then walk to the end of the lead. Correct him strongly if he starts to move. Have a stranger approach him and run his hands over the dog's back and down his legs. Keep him standing until you come back to him. Walk around him from his left side, come to the heel position, and make sure that he does not sit until you command him to.

This is a very valuable exercise. If you plan to show your dog he will have learned to stand in a show pose and will allow the judge to examine him.

TRAINING SCHOOLS AND CLASSES

There are dog-training classes in all parts of the country, some sponsored by the local humane society.

If you feel that you lack the time or the skill to train your dog yourself, there are professional dog trainers who will do it for you, but basically dog training is a matter of training YOU and your dog to work together as a team, and if you don't do it yourself you will miss a lot of fun. Don't give up after trying unsuccessfully for a short time. Try a little harder and you and your dog will be able to work things out.

ADVANCED TRAINING AND OBEDIENCE TRIALS

Once you begin training your dog and you see how well he does, you'll probably be bitten by the "obedience bug" — the desire to enter him in obedience trials held under American Kennel Club auspices.

The A.K.C. obedience trials are divided into three classes: Novice, Open, and Utility.

In the Novice Class, the dog will be judged on the following basis:

TEST	MAXIMUM SCORE
Heel on lead	35
Stand for examination	30
Heel free — off lead	45
Recall (come on command)	30
One-minute sit (handler in ring)	30
Three-minute down (handler in ring)	30
Maximum total score	200

40

If the dog "qualifies" in three shows by earning at least 50% of the points for each test, with a total of at least 170 for the trial, he has earned the Companion Dog degree and the letters C.D. (Companion Dog) are entered after his name in the A.K.C. records.

After the dog has qualified as a C.D., he is eligible to enter the Open Class competition, where he will be judged on this basis:

TEST	MAXIMUM SCORE
Heel free	40
Drop on Recall	30
Retrieve (wooden dumbbell) on flat	25
Retrieve over obstacle (hurdle)	35
Broad jump	20
Three-minute sit (handler out of ring)	25
Five-minute down (handler out of ring)	25
Maximum total score	200

Again he must qualify in three shows for the C.D.X. (Companion Dog Excellent) title and then is eligible for the Utility Class, where he can earn the Utility Dog (U.D.) degree in these rugged tests:

TEST	MAXIMUM SCORE
Scent discrimination (picking up article handled by master from group) Article 1	20
Scent discrimination Article 2	20
Scent discrimination Article 3	20
Seek back (picking up an article dropped by handler)	30
Signal exercise (heeling, etc., on hand signal)	35
Directed jumping (over hurdle and bar jump)	40
Group examination	35
Maximum total score	200

For more complete information about these obedience trials, write for the American Kennel Club's *Regulations and Standards for Obedience Trials*. Dogs that are disqualified from breed shows because of alteration or physical defects are eligible to compete in these trials. Besides the formal A.K.C. obedience trials, there are informal "match" shows in which dogs compete for ribbons and inexpensive trophies. These shows are run by many local fanciers' dog clubs and by all-breed obedience clubs. In many localities the humane society and other groups conduct their own obedience shows. Your local petshop or kennel can keep you informed about such shows in your vicinity, and you will find them listed in the different dog magazines or in the pet column of your local newspaper.

6. Breeding

THE QUESTION OF SPAYING

If you feel that you will never want to raise a litter of purebred puppies, and if you do not wish to risk the possibility of an undesirable mating and surplus mongrel puppies inevitably destined for execution at the local pound, you may want to have your female spayed. Spaying is generally best performed after the female has passed her first heat and before her first birthday: this allows the female to attain the normal female characteristics, while still being young enough to avoid the possible complications encountered when an older female is spayed. A spayed female will remain a healthy, lively pet. You often hear that an altered female will become very fat. However, if you cut down on her food intake, she will not gain weight.

On the other hand, if you wish to show your dog (altered females are disqualified) or enjoy the excitement and feeling of accomplishment of breeding and raising a litter of puppies, particularly in your breed and from your pet, then definitely do not spay.

Male dogs, unlike tomcats, are almost never altered (castrated).

SEXUAL PHYSIOLOGY

Females usually reach sexual maturity (indicated by the first heat cycle, or season) at eight or nine months of age, but sexual maturity may occur as early as six months or as late as thirteen months of age. The average heat cycle (estrus period) lasts for twenty or twenty-one days, and occurs approximately every six months. For about five days immediately preceding the heat period, the female generally displays restlessness and an increased appetite. The vulva, or external genitals, begin to swell. The discharge, which is bright red at the onset and gradually becomes pale pink to straw in color, increases in quantity for several days and then slowly subsides, finally ceasing altogether. The vaginal discharge is subject to much variation: in some bitches it is quite heavy, in others it may never appear, and in some it may be so slight as to go unnoticed.

About eight or nine days after the first appearance of the discharge, the female becomes very playful with other dogs, but will not allow a mating to take place. Anywhere from the tenth or eleventh day, when the discharge has virtually ended and the vulva has softened, to the seventeenth or eighteenth day, the female will accept males and be able to conceive. Many biologists apply the term "heat" only to this receptive phase rather than to the whole estrus, as is commonly done by dog fanciers.

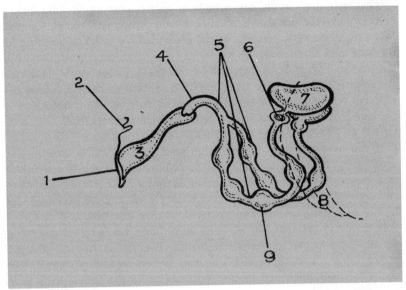

The reproduction system of the bitch: 1, vulva; 2, anus; 3, vagina; 4, cervix; 5, uterus; 6, ovary; 7, kidneys; 8, ribs; 9, fetal lump.

The ova (egg cells) from the female's ovaries are discharged into the oviduct toward the close of the acceptance phase, usually from the sixteenth to eighteenth day. From the eighteenth day until the end of the cycle, the female is still attractive to males, but she will repulse their advances. The entire estrus, however, may be quite variable: in some females vaginal bleeding ends and mating begins on the fourth day; in others, the discharge may continue throughout the entire cycle and the female will not accept males until the seventeenth day or even later.

The male dog — simply referred to by fanciers as the "dog," in contrast to the female, which is referred to as the "bitch" — upon reaching sexual maturity, usually at about six to eight months, is able, like other domesticated mammals, to breed at any time throughout the year.

The testes, the sperm-producing organs of the male, descend from the body cavity into the scrotum at birth. The condition of *cryptorchidism* refers to the retention of one or both testes within the body cavity. A testicle retained within the body cavity is in an environment too hot for it to function normally. A retained testicle may also become cancerous. If only one testicle descends, the dog is known as a *monorchid;* if neither descends, the dog is known as an *anorchid* (dog fanciers, however, refer to a dog with the latter condition as a cryptorchid). A monorchid dog is a fertile animal; an anorchid is sterile.

The male dog's penis has a bulbous enlargement at its base and, in addition, like the penis of a number of other mammals, contains a bone. When mating occurs, pressure on the penis causes a reflex action that fills the bulb with blood, swelling it to about five times its normal size within the female. This locks, or ties, the two animals together. After ejaculation, the animals usually remain tied for fifteen to thirty minutes, but they may separate very quickly or remain together an hour or more, depending on the length of time it takes for the blood to drain from the bulb.

CARE OF THE FEMALE IN ESTRUS

If you have a dog-proof run within your yard, it will be safe to leave your female in season there; if you don't have such a run, she should be shut indoors. Don't leave her alone outside even for a minute; she should be exercised only on lead. If you want to prevent the neighborhood dogs from congregating around your doorstep, as they inevitably will as soon as they discover that your female is in season, take her some distance from the house before you let her relieve herself. Take her in your car to a park or field for a chance to "stretch" her legs (always on lead of course). Keep watch for male dogs, and if one approaches take the female back to the car. After the three weeks are up you can let her out as before with no worry that she can have puppies until her next season.

Some owners find it simpler to board their female at a kennel until her season is over. However, it really is not difficult to watch your female at home. There are various products on the market which are useful at this time. Although the female in season keeps herself quite clean, sometimes she unavoidably stains furniture or rugs. You can buy sanitary belts made especially for dogs at your petshop. Consult your veterinarian for information on pills to be taken to check odor during this period. There also is a pill that prevents the female from coming in season for extended periods, and there are many different types of liquids, powders, and sprays of varying efficiency used to keep male dogs away. However, the one safe rule (whatever products you use) is: keep your bitch away from dogs that could mount her.

SHOULD YOU BREED YOUR MALE?

As with every question, whether or not to use a male dog as a stud has two sides. The arguments for and against using a dog as a stud are often very close to the ridiculous. A classic example would be the tale that once you use a dog as a stud he will lose his value as a show dog or any one of the other functions a dog may have. A sound rule may well be: *if you have a stud who has proven his worth at the shows, place his services out for hire, if only for the betterment of the breed; if your dog is not of show quality, do not use him as a stud.*

Top champion studs can bring their owners many dollars in breeding revenue. If the stud is as good as you feel he is, his services will soon be in great demand. Using a dog as a stud will not lower his value in other functions in any way. Many breeders will permit a male dog to breed an experienced female once, when about a year old, and then they begin to show their stud until he has gained his conformation championship. He is then placed out for hire through advertising in the various bulletins, journals, and show catalogs, and through the stud registers maintained by many pet-shops.

SHOULD YOU BREED YOUR FEMALE?

If you are an amateur and decide to breed your female it would be wise to talk with a breeder and find out all that breeding and caring for puppies entails. You must be prepared to assume the responsibility of caring for the mother through her pregnancy and for the puppies until they are of saleable age. Raising a litter of puppies can be a rewarding experience, but it means work as well as fun, and there is no guarantee of financial profit. As the puppies grow older and require more room and care, the amateur breeder, in desperation, often sells the puppies for much less than they are worth; sometimes he has to give them away. If the cost of keeping the puppies will drain your finances, think twice.

If you have given careful consideration to all these things and still want to breed your female, remember that there is some preparation necessary before taking this step.

WHEN TO BREED

It is usually best to breed in the second or third season. Consider when the puppies will be born and whether their birth and later care will inter-fere with your work or vacation plans. Gestation period is approximately fifty-eight to sixty-three days. Allow enough time to select the right stud for her. Don't be in a position of having to settle for any available male if she comes into season sooner than expected. Your female will probably be ready to breed twelve days after the first colored discharge. You can usually make arrangements to board her with the owner of the male for a few days to insure her being there at the proper time, or you can take her to be mated and bring her home the same day. If she still appears receptive she may be bred again a day or two later. Some females never show signs of willingness, so it helps to have the experience of a breeder. The second day after the discharge changes color is the proper time; she may be bred for about three days following. For an additional week or so she may have some discharge and attract other dogs by her odor, but she can seldom be bred at this time.

HOW TO SELECT A STUD

Choose a mate for your female with an eye to countering her deficiencies. If possible, both male and female should have several ancestors in common within the last two or three generations, as such combinations generally "click" best. The male should have a good show record himself or be the sire of champions. The owner of the stud usually charges a fee for the use of the dog. The fee varies. Payment of a fee does not guarantee a litter, but it does generally confer the right to breed your female again to the stud if she does not have puppies the first time. In some cases the owner of the stud will agree to take a choice puppy in place of a stud fee. You and the owner of the stud should settle all details beforehand, including such questions as what age the puppies should reach before the stud's owner can make his choice, what disposition is made of a single surviving puppy under an agreement by which the stud owner has pick of the litter, and so on. In all cases it is best that the agreement entered into by bitch owner and stud owner be in the form of a written contract.

It is customary for the female to be sent to the male; if the stud dog of your choice lives any distance you will have to make arrangements to have your female shipped to him. The quickest way is by air, and if you call your nearest airport the airline people will give you information as to the best and fastest flight. Some airlines furnish their own crates for shipping, whereas others require that you furnish your own. The owner of the stud will make the arrangements for shipping the female back to you. You have to pay all shipping charges.

PREPARATION FOR BREEDING

Before you breed your female, make sure she is in good health. She should be neither too thin nor too fat. Skin diseases must be cured before breeding; a bitch with skin diseases can pass them on to her puppies. If she has worms she should be wormed before being bred, or within three weeks afterward. It is a good idea to have your veterinarian give her a booster shot for distemper and hepatitis before the puppies are born. This will increase the immunity the puppies receive during their early, most vulnerable period. Choose a dependable veterinarian and rely on him if there is an emergency when your female whelps.

HOW OFTEN SHOULD YOU BREED YOUR FEMALE?

Do not breed your bitch after she reaches six years of age. If you wish to breed her several times while she is young, it is wise to breed her only once a year. In other words, breed her, skip a season, and then breed her again. This will allow her to gain back her full strength between whelpings.

THE IMPORTANCE AND APPLICATION OF GENETICS

Any person attempting to breed dogs should have a basic understanding of the transmission of traits, or characteristics, from the parents to the offspring and some familiarity with the more widely used genetic terms that he will probably encounter. A knowledge of the fundamental mechanics of genetics enables a breeder to better comprehend the passing, complementing, and covering of both good points and faults from generation to generation. It enables him to make a more judicial and scientific decision in selecting potential mates.

Inheritance, fundamentally, is due to the existence of microscopic units, known as *GENES,* present in the cells of all individuals. Genes somehow control the biochemical reactions that occur within the embryo or adult organism. This control results in changing or guiding the development of the organism's characteristics. A "string" of attached genes is known as a *CHROMOSOME.* With a few important exceptions, every chromosome has a partner chromosome carrying a duplicate or equivalent set of genes. Each gene, therefore, has a partner gene, known as an *ALLELE.* The number of different pairs of chromosomes present in the cells of the organism varies with the type of organism: a certain parasitic worm has only one pair, a certain fruit fly has four different pairs, man has 23 different pairs, and your dog has 39 different pairs per cell. Because each chromosome may have many hundreds of genes, a single cell of the body may contain a total of several thousand genes. Heredity is obviously a very complex matter.

In the simplest form of genetic inheritance, one particular gene and its duplicate, or allele, on the partner chromosome control a single characteristic. The presence of freckles in the human skin, for example, is believed to be due to the influence of a single pair of genes.

Each cell of the body contains the specific number of paired chromosomes characteristic of the organism. Because each type of gene is present on both chromosomes of a chromosome pair, *each type of gene is therefore present in duplicate.* The fusion of a sperm cell from the male with an egg cell from the female, as occurs in fertilization, should therefore result in offspring having a *quadruplicate number* (4) of each type of gene. Mating of these individuals would then produce progeny having an *octuplicate number* (8) of each type of gene, and so on. This, however, is normally prevented by a special process. When ordinary body cells prepare to divide to form more tissue, each pair of chromosomes duplicates itself so that there are four partner chromosomes of each kind instead of only two. When the cell divides, two of the four partners, or one pair, go into each new cell. This process, known as *MITOSIS,* insures that each new body cell contains the proper number of chromosomes. Reproductive cells (sperm cell and egg cells), however, undergo a special kind of division known as *MEIOSIS.* In meiosis, the chromosome pairs do *not* duplicate themselves, and thus when the reproductive cells reach the final dividing stage only one chromosome, or one-half of the pair, goes into each new reproductive cell. Each reproductive cell, therefore, has only half the normal number of chromosomes. These are referred to as *HAPLOID* cells, in contrast to *DIPLOID* cells, which have the full number of chromosomes.

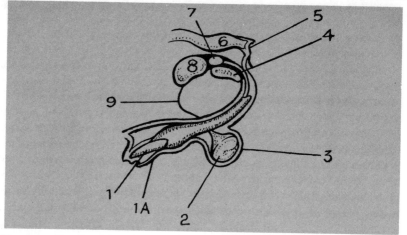

The reproductive system of a male: 1a, sheath; 1, penis; 2, testicle; 3, scrotum; 4, pelvic bone; 5, anus; 6, rectum; 7, prostate; 8, bladder; 9, vas deferens.

When the haploid sperm cell fuses with the haploid egg cell in fertilization, the resulting offspring has the normal diploid number of chromosomes.

If both partner genes, or alleles, affect the trait in an identical manner, the genes are said to be *HOMOZYGOUS*, but if one affects the character in a manner different from the other gene, or allele, the genes are said to be *HETEROZYGOUS*. For example, in the pair of genes affecting eye color in humans, if each gene of the pair produces blue eyes, the genes (and also the person carrying the genes) are said to be homozygous for blue eyes. If, however, one gene of the pair produces blue eyes, while the other gene, or allele, produces brown eyes, they are said to be heterozygous. The presence of heterozygous genes raises the question, *"Will the offspring have blue eyes or brown eyes?"* which in turn introduces another genetic principle: *DOMINANCE* and *RECESSIVENESS*.

If one gene of a pair can block the action of its partner, or allele, while still producing its own affect, that gene is said to be *dominant* over its allele. Its allele, on the other hand, is said to be recessive. In the case of heterozygous genes for eye color, the brown eye gene is dominant over the recessive blue eye gene, and the offspring therefore will have brown eyes. Much less common is the occurrence of gene pairs in which neither gene is completely dominant over the other. This, known as *INCOMPLETE* or *PARTIAL DOMINANCE*, results in a blending of the opposing influences. In cattle, if a homozygous (pure) red bull is mated with a homozygous (pure) white cow, the calf will be roan, a blending of red and white hairs in its coat, rather than either all red or all white.

During meiosis, or division of the reproductive (sperm and egg) cells, each pair of chromosomes splits, and one-half of each pair goes into one of the two new cells. Thus, in the case of eye color genes, one new reproductive cell will get the chromosome carrying the blue eye gene, while the other new reproductive cell will get the chromosome carrying the brown eye gene, and so on for each pair of chromosomes. If an organism has only two pairs of chromosomes — called pair A, made up of chromosomes A_1 and A_2, and pair B, made up of chromosomes B_1 and B_2 — each new reproductive cell will get one chromosome from each pair, and four different combinations are possible: A_1 and B_1; A_1 and B_2; A_2 and B_1, or A_2 and B_2. If the blue eye gene is on A_1, the brown eye gene on A_2, the gene for curly hair on B_1 and the gene for straight hair on B_2, each of the above combinations will exert a different genetic effect on the offspring. This different grouping of chromosomes in the new reproductive cell as a result of meiotic cell division is known as *INDEPENDENT ASSORTMENT* and is one reason why variation occurs in the offspring. In the dog, with 39 pairs of chromosomes, the possibilities of variation through independent assortment are tremendous.

But variation does not end here. For example, if two dominant genes, such as the genes for brown eyes and dark hair, were on the same chromosome, all brown-eyed people would have dark hair. Yet in instances where such joined or *LINKED* genes do occur, the two characteristics do not always appear together in the same offspring. This is due to a process known as *CROSS-OVER* or *RECOMBINATION*. Recombination is the mutual exchange of corresponding blocks of genes between the two chromosomes in a pair. That is, during cell division, the two chromosomes may exchange their tip sections or other corresponding segments. If the segments exchanged contain the eye color genes, the brown eye gene will be transferred from the chromosome carrying the dark hair gene to the chromosome carrying the light hair gene, and then brown eyes will occur with light hair, provided that the individual is homozygous for the recessive light hair gene.

Another important source of variation is *MUTATION*. In mutation, a gene becomes altered, such as by exposure to irradiation, and exerts a different effect than it did before. Most mutations are harmful to the organism, and some may result in death. Offspring carrying mutated genes and showing the effects of these mutations are known as *MUTANTS* or *SPORTS*. Mutation also means that instead of only two alleles for eye color, such as brown and blue, there may now be three or more (gray, black, etc.) creating a much larger source for possible variation in the offspring.

Further complications in the transmission and appearance of genetic traits are the phenomena known as *EPISTASIS* and *PLEIOTROPY*. Epistasis refers to a gene exerting influence on genes other than its own allele.

In all-white red-eyed (albino) guinea pigs, for example, the gene controlling intensity of color is epistatic to any other color gene and prevents that gene from producing its effect. Thus, even if a gene for red spots were present in the cells of the guinea pig, the color intensity gene would prevent the red spots from appearing in the guinea pig's white coat. *Pleiotropy* refers to the fact that a single gene may control a number of characteristics. In the fruit fly, for example, the gene that controls eye color may also affect the structure of certain body parts and even the lifespan of the insect.

One special pair of chromosomes is known as the sex chromosomes. In man, dog, and other mammals, these chromosomes are of two types, designated as X and Y. Under normal conditions, a mammal carrying two X-type sex chromosomes is a female, whereas a mammal carrying one X-type and one Y-type is a male. Females, therefore, have only X chromosomes and can only contribute X chromosomes to the offspring, but the male may contribute either an X or a Y.

If the male's sperm carrying an X chromosome fertilizes the female's egg cell (X), the offspring (XX) will be female; if a sperm carrying a Y chromosome fertilizes the egg (X), the offspring (XY) will be male. It is the male, therefore, that determines the sex of the offspring in mammals.

Traits controlled by genes present on the sex chromosome, and which appear in only one sex, are said to be *SEX LINKED*. If, for example, a rare recessive gene occurs on the X chromosome, it cannot exert its effect in the female because the dominant allele on the other X chromosome will counteract it. In the male, however, there is no second X chromosome, and if the Y chromosome cannot offer any countereffect, the recessive character will appear. There are also *SEX-LIMITED* characteristics: these appear primarily or solely in one sex, but the genes for these traits are not carried on the sex chromosomes. Sex-limited traits appear when genes on other chromosomes exert their effect in the proper hormonal (male or female) environment. Sex-linked and sex-limited transmission is how a trait may skip a generation, by being passed from grandfather to grandson through a mother in which the trait, though present, does not show.

In dealing with the simplest form of heredity — one gene effecting one character — there is an expected ratio of the offspring displaying the character to those who do not display it, depending upon the genetic makeup of the parents. If a parent is homozygous for a character, such as blue eyes, it makes no difference which half of the chromosome pair enters the new reproductive cell, because each chromosome carries the gene for blue eyes. If a parent is heterozygous, however, one reproductive cell will receive the brown eye gene while the other will receive the blue eye gene. If both parents are homozygous for blue eyes, all the offspring will receive two blue eye genes, and all will have blue eyes. If a parent is homozygous for blue eyes, and the other parent is homozygous for brown eyes, all the offspring will be heterozygous, receiving one brown eye gene and one blue eye gene, and because brown is dominant, all will have brown eyes. If both parents are heterozygous, both the blue eye gene and the brown eye gene from one parent have an equal likelihood of ending up with either the blue eye or the brown eye gene from the other parent. This results in a ratio of two heterozygous offspring to the one homozygous for brown eyes and one homozygous for blue eyes, giving a total genetic, or genotypic, ratio of $2:1:1$ or, as it is more commonly arranged, $1:2:1$. As the two heterozygous as well as the homozygous brown eye offspring will have brown eyes, the ratio of brown eyes to blue eyes (or phenotypic ratio) will be $3:1$.

If one parent is heterozygous and the other parent is homozygous for the recessive gene for blue eyes, half of the offspring will be homozygous for blue eyes and will have blue eyes, but the other half of the offspring will be heterozygous and have brown eyes. (Here both the genotypic and phenotypic ratio is $1:1$.)

If the homozygous parent, however, has the dominant gene (brown eyes), half of the offspring will be heterozygous and half will be homozygous, as before, but all will have brown eyes. By repeated determinations of these ratios in the offspring, geneticists are able to analyze the genetic makeup of the parents.

Before leaving heredity, it might be well to explain the difference between inbreeding, outcrossing, line breeding, and similar terms. Basically, there are only inbreeding and outbreeding. Inbreeding, however, according to its intensity, is usually divided into inbreeding proper and line breeding. Inbreeding proper is considered to be the mating of very closely related individuals, generally within the immediate family, but this is sometimes extended to include matings to first cousins and grandparents. Line breeding is the mating of more distantly related animals, that is, animals, not immediately related to each other but having a common ancestor, such as the same grandsire or great-grandsire. Outbreeding is divided into outcrossing, which is the mating of dogs from different families within the same breed, and cross-breeding, which is mating purebred dogs from different breeds.

From the foregoing discussion of genetics, it should be realized that the theory of telegony, which states that the sire of one litter can influence future litters sired by other studs, is simply not true; it is possible, however, if several males mate with a female during a single estrus cycle, that the various puppies in the litter may have different sires (but not two sires for any one puppy). It should also be realized that blood does not really enter into the transmission of inheritance, although people commonly speak of "bloodlines," "pure-blooded," etc.

7. Care of the Mother and Family

PRENATAL CARE OF THE FEMALE

You can expect the puppies nine weeks from the day of breeding, although 58 days is as common as 63. During this time the female should receive normal care and exercise. If she is overweight, don't increase her food at first; excess weight at whelping time is not good. If she is on the thin side, build her up, giving her a morning meal of cereal and egg yolk. Consult your veterinarian as to increasing her vitamins and mineral supplement. During the last weeks the puppies grow enormously, and the mother will have little room for food and less appetite. Divide her meals into smaller portions and feed her more ofen. If she loses her appetite, tempt her with meat, liver, chicken, etc.

As she grows heavier, eliminate violent exercise and jumping. Do not eliminate exercise entirely, as walking is beneficial to the female in whelp, and mild exercise will maintain her muscle tone in preparation for the birth. Weigh your female after breeding and keep a record of her weight each week thereafter. Groom your bitch daily — some females have a slight discharge during gestation, more prevalent during the last two weeks, so wash the vulva with warm water daily. Usually, by the end of the fifth week you can notice a broadening across her loins, and her breasts become firmer. By the end of the sixth week your veterinarian can tell you whether or not she is pregnant.

PREPARATION OF WHELPING QUARTERS

Prepare a whelping box at least a week before the puppies are to arrive and allow the mother-to-be to sleep there overnight or to spend some time in it during the day to become accustomed to it. She is then less likely to try to have her litter under the front porch or in the middle of your bed.

The box should have a wooden floor. Sides should be high enough to keep the puppies in but low enough to allow the mother to get out after she has fed them. Layers of newspapers spread over the whole area will make excellent bedding and will be absorbent enough to keep the surface warm and dry. They should be removed when wet or soiled and replaced with another thick layer. An old quilt or blanket is more comfortable for the mother and makes better footing for the nursing puppies, at least during the first week, than slippery newspaper. The quilt should be secured firmly.

SUPPLIES TO HAVE ON HAND

As soon as you have the whelping box prepared, set up the nursery by collecting the various supplies you will need when the puppies arrive. You should have the following items on hand: a box lined with towels for the puppies, a heating pad or hot water bottle to keep the puppy box warm, a pile of clean terrycloth towels or washcloths to remove membranes and to dry puppies, a stack of folded newspapers, a roll of paper towels, vaseline, rubber gloves, soap, iodine, muzzle, cotton balls, a small pair of blunt scissors to cut umbilical cords (stick them into an open bottle of alcohol so they keep freshly sterilized), a rectal thermometer, white thread, a flashlight in case the electricity goes off, a waste container, and a scale for weighing each puppy at birth.

It is necessary that the whelping room be warm and free from drafts, because puppies are delivered wet from the mother. Keep a little notebook and pencil handy so you can record the duration of the first labor and the time between the arrival of each puppy. If there is trouble in whelping, this is the information that the veterinarian will want. Keep his telephone number handy in case you have to call him in an emergency, and warn him to be prepared for an emergency, should you need him.

WHELPING

Be prepared for the actual whelping several days in advance. Usually the female will tear up papers, try to dig nests, refuse food, and generally act restless and nervous. These may be false alarms; the real test is her temperature, which will drop to below 100° about twelve hours before whelping. Take her temperature rectally at a set time each day, starting about a week before she is due to whelp. After her temperature goes down, keep her constantly with you or put her in the whelping box and stay in the room with her. She will seem anxious and look to you for reassurance. Be prepared to remove the membranes covering the puppy's head if the mother fails to do this, for the puppy could smother otherwise.

The mother should start licking the puppy as soon as it is out of the sac, thus drying and stimulating it, but if she does not perform this task you can do it with a soft rough towel, instead. The afterbirth should follow the birth of each puppy, attached to the puppy by the umbilical cord. Watch to make sure that each is expelled, for retaining this material can cause infection. The mother probably will eat the afterbirth after biting the cord. One or two will not hurt her; they stimulate milk supply as well as labor for remaining puppies. Too many, however, can make her lose her appetite for the food she needs to feed her puppies and regain her strength, so remove the rest of them along with the soiled newspapers, and keep the box dry and clean to relieve her anxiety.

If a puppy does not start breathing, wrap him in a towel, hold him upside down with his head toward the ground, and shake him vigorously. If he still does not breathe, rub his ribs briskly; if this also fails, administer artificial respiration by compressing the ribs about twenty times per minute.

If the mother does not bite the cord, or bites it too close to the body, you should take over the job to prevent an umbilical hernia. Cut the cord a short distance from the body with your blunt scissors. Put a drop of iodine on the end of the cord; it will dry up and fall off in a few days.

The puppies should follow each other at regular intervals, but deliveries can be as short as five minutes or as long as two hours apart. A puppy may be presented backwards; if the mother does not seem to be in trouble, do not interfere. But if enough of the puppy is outside the birth canal, use a rough towel and help her by pulling gently on the puppy. Pull only when she pushes. A rear-first, or breech, birth can cause a puppy to strangle on its own umbilical cord, so don't let the mother struggle too long. Breech birth is quite common.

When you think all the puppies have been whelped, have your veterinarian examine the mother to determine if all the afterbirths have been expelled. He will probably give her an injection to be certain that the uterus is clean, a shot of calcium for prevention of eclampsia, and possibly an injection of penicillin to prevent infection.

RAISING THE PUPPIES

Hold each puppy to a breast as soon as you have dried him. This will be an opportunity to have a good meal without competition. Then place him in the small box that you have prepared so he will be out of his mother's way while she is whelping. Keep a record of birth weights and take weekly readings thereafter so that you will have an accurate account of the puppies' growth. After the puppies have arrived, take the mother outside for a walk and a drink, and then leave her to take care of them. Offer her a dish of vanilla ice cream or milk with corn syrup in it. She usually will eat lying down while the puppies are nursing and will appreciate the coolness of the ice cream during warm weather or in a hot room. She will not want to stay away from her puppies more than a minute or two the first few weeks. Be sure to keep water available at all times, and feed her milk or broth frequently, as she needs liquids to produce milk. To encourage her to eat, offer her the foods she likes best, until she "asks" to be fed without your tempting her. She will soon develop a ravenous appetite and should be fed whenever she is hungry.

Be sure that all the puppies are getting enough to eat. Cut their claws with special dog "nail" clippers, as they grow rapidly and scratch the mother as the puppies nurse. Normally the puppies should be completely weaned by six weeks, although you may start to give them supplementary feedings at three weeks. They will find it easier to lap semi-solid food.

As the puppies grow up, the mother will go into the box only to nurse them, first sitting up and then standing. To dry up her milk supply completely, keep her away from her puppies for longer periods. After a few days of part-time nursing she will be able to stay away for much longer periods of time, and then completely. The little milk left will be resorbed.

When the puppies are five weeks old, consult your veterinarian about temporary shots to protect them against distemper and hepatitis; it is quite possible for dangerous infectious germs to reach them even though you keep their living quarters sanitary. You can expect the puppies to need at least one worming before they are ready to go to their new homes, so take a stool sample to your veterinarian before they are three weeks old. If one puppy has worms, all should be wormed. Follow your veterinarian's advice.

The puppies may be put outside, unless it is too cold, as soon as their eyes are open (about ten days), and they will benefit from the sunlight. A rubber mat or newspapers underneath their box will protect them from cold or dampness.

HOW TO TAKE CARE OF A LARGE LITTER

The size of a litter varies greatly. If your bitch has a large litter she may have trouble feeding all of the puppies. You can help her by preparing an extra puppy box. Leave half the litter with the mother and the other half in a warm place, changing their places at two-hour intervals at first. Later you may change them less frequently, leaving them all together except during the day. Try supplementary feeding, too, as soon as their eyes are open.

CAESAREAN SECTION

If your female goes into hard labor and is not able to give birth within two hours, you will know that there is something wrong. Call your veterinarian for advice. Some females must have Caesarean sections (taking puppies from the mother by surgery), but don't be alarmed if your dog has to undergo this. The operation is relatively safe. She can be taken to the veterinarian, operated on, and then be back in her whelping box at home within three hours, with all puppies nursing normally a short time later.

8. Health

WATCHING YOUR PUPPY'S HEALTH

First, don't be frightened by the number of diseases a dog can contract. The majority of dogs never get any of them. Don't become a dog-hypochondriac. All dogs have days when they feel lazy and want to lie around doing nothing. For the few diseases that you might be concerned about, remember that your veterinarian is your dog's best friend. When you first get your puppy, select a veterinarian who you feel is qualified to treat dogs. He will get to know your dog and will be glad to have you consult him for advice. A dog needs little medical care, but that little is essential to his good health and well-being. He needs:

1. Proper diet at regular hours
2. Clean, roomy housing
3. Daily exercise
4. Companionship and love
5. Frequent grooming
6. Regular check-ups by your veterinarian

THE USEFUL THERMOMETER

Almost every serious ailment shows itself by an increase in the dog's body temperature. If your dog acts lifeless, looks dull-eyed, and gives the impression of illness, check his temperature by using a rectal thermometer. Hold the dog and insert the thermometer, which should be lubricated with vaseline, and take a reading. The average normal temperature is 101.5° F. Excitement may raise this value slightly, but any rise of more than a few points is a cause for alarm. Consult your veterinarian.

FIRST AID

In general, a dog will heal his wounds by licking them. If he swallows anything harmful, chances are that he will throw it up. But it will probably make you feel better to help him if he is hurt, so treat his wounds as you would your own. Wash out the dirt and apply an antiseptic. If you are afraid that your dog has swallowed poison and you can't get to the veterinarian fast enough, try to induce vomiting by giving him a strong solution of salt water or mustard and water. Amateur diagnosis is dangerous, because the symptoms of so many dog diseases are alike. Too many people wait too long to take their dog to the doctor.

IMPORTANCE OF INOCULATIONS

With the proper series of inoculations, your dog will be almost completely protected against disease. However, it occasionally happens that the shot does not take, and sometimes a different form of the virus appears against which your dog may not be protected.

DISTEMPER

Probably the most virulent of all dog diseases is distemper. Young dogs are most susceptible to it, although it may affect dogs of all ages. The dog will lose his appetite, seem depressed, chilled, and run a fever. Often he will have a watery discharge from his eyes and nose. Unless treated promptly, the disease goes into advanced stages with infections of the lungs, intestines, and nervous system, and dogs that recover may be left with some impairment such as paralysis, convulsions, a twitch, or some other defect, usually spastic in nature. The best protection against this is very early inoculation with a series of permanent shots and a booster shot each year thereafter.

HEPATITIS

Veterinarians report an increase in the spread of this viral disease in recent years, usually with younger dogs as the victims. The initial symptoms — drowsiness, vomiting, great thirst, loss of appetite, and a high temperature — closely resemble those of distemper. These symptoms are often accompanied by swellings of the head, neck, and abdomen. The disease strikes quickly; death may occur in just a few hours. Protection is afforded by injection with a vaccine recently developed.

LEPTOSPIROSIS

This disease is caused by bacteria that live in stagnant or slow-moving water. It is carried by rats and dogs; infection is begun by the dog's licking substances contaminated by the urine or feces of infected animals. The symptoms are diarrhea and a yellowish-brown discoloration of the jaws, tongue, and teeth, caused by an inflammation of the kidneys. This disease can be cured if caught in time, but it is best to ward it off with a vaccine which your veterinarian can administer along with the distemper shots.

RABIES

This is an acute disease of the dog's central nervous system. It is spread by infectious saliva transmitted by the bite of an infected animal. Rabies is generally manifested in one of two classes of symptoms. The first is "furious rabies," in which the dog shows a period of melancholy or depression, then irritation, and finally paralysis. The first period lasts from a few hours to several days. During this time the dog is cross and will change his position often. He loses his appetite for food and begins to lick, bite, and swallow foreign objects. During the irritative phase the dog is spasmodically wild and has impulses to run away. He acts in a fearless manner and runs and bites at everything in sight. If he is caged or confined he will fight at the bars, often breaking teeth or fracturing his jaw. His bark becomes a peculiar howl. In the final, or paralytic, stage, the animal's lower jaw becomes paralyzed and hangs down; he walks with a stagger and saliva drips from his mouth. Within four to eight days after the onset of paralysis, the dog dies.

The second class of symptoms is referred to as "dumb rabies" and is characterized by the dog's walking in a bearlike manner, head down. The lower jaw is paralyzed and the dog is unable to bite. Outwardly it may seem as though he had a bone caught in his throat.

Even if your pet should be bitten by a rabid dog or other animal, he probably can be saved if you get him to the veterinarian in time for a series of injections. However, after the symptoms have appeared no cure is possible. But remember that an annual rabies inoculation is almost certain protection against rabies. If you suspect your dog of rabies, notify your local Health Department. A rabid dog is a danger to all who come near him.

COUGHS, COLDS, BRONCHITIS, PNEUMONIA

Respiratory diseases may affect the dog because he is forced to live under man-made conditions rather than in his natural environment. Being subjected to cold or a draft after a bath, sleeping near an air conditioner or in the path of a fan or near a radiator can cause respiratory ailments. The symptoms are similar to those in humans. The germs of these diseases, however, are different and do not affect both dogs and humans, so they cannot be infected by each other. Treatment is much the same as for a child with the same type of illness. Keep the dog warm, quiet, and well fed. Your veterinarian has antibiotics and other remedies to help the dog recover.

INTERNAL PARASITES

There are four common internal parasites that may infect your dog. These are roundworms, hookworms, whipworms, and tapeworms. The first three can be diagnosed by laboratory examination; the presence of tapeworms is determined by seeing segments in the stool or attached to the hair around the tail. Do not under any circumstances attempt to worm your dog without the advice of your veterinarian. After first determining what type of worm or worms are present, he will advise you of the best method of treatment.

EXTERNAL PARASITES

The dog that is groomed regularly and provided with clean sleeping quarters should not be troubled by fleas, ticks, or lice. If the dog should become infested with any of these parasites, he should be treated with a medicated dip bath or the new oral medications that are presently available.

SKIN AILMENTS

Any persistent scratching may indicate an irritation. Whenever you groom your dog, look for the reddish spots that may indicate eczema, mange, or fungal infection. Rather than treating your dog yourself, take him to the

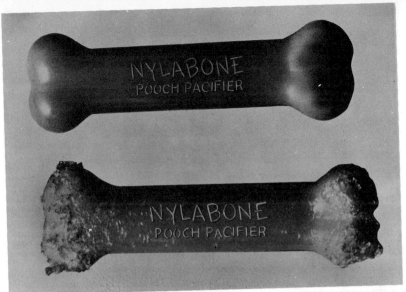

NYLABONE® is a necessity that is available at your local petshop (not in supermarkets). The puppy or grown dog chews the hambone flavored nylon into a frilly dog toothbrush, massaging his gums and cleaning his teeth as he plays. Veterinarians highly recommend this product . . . but beware of cheap imitations which might splinter or break.

veterinarian, as some of the conditions may be difficult to eradicate and can cause permanent damage to his coat.

EYES, EARS, TEETH, AND CLAWS

If you notice foreign matter collecting in the corners of your dog's eyes, wipe it out with a piece of cotton or tissue. If there is a discharge, check with your veterinarian.

Examine your dog's ears daily. Remove all visible wax, using a piece of cotton dipped in a boric acid solution or a solution of equal parts of water and hydrogen peroxide. Be gentle and don't probe into the ear, but just clean the parts you can see.

Don't give your dog bones to chew: they can choke him or puncture his intestines. Today veterinarians and dog experts recommend Nylabone, a synthetic bone manufactured by a secret process, that can't splinter or break even when pounded by a hammer. Nylabone will keep puppies from chewing furniture, aid in relieving the aching gums of a teething pup, and act as a toothbrush for the older dog, preventing the accumulation of tartar. Check your dog's mouth regularly and, as he gets older, have your veterinarian clean his teeth twice a year.

To clip your dog's claws, use specially designed clippers that are available at your petshop. Never take off too much of the claw, as you might

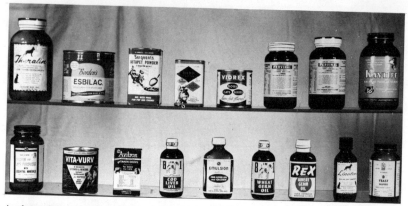

Active dogs and breeding bitches need food supplements. Visit your petshop for fresh vitamins and minerals to be added to your dog's diet.

cut the quick, which is sensitive and will bleed. Be particularly careful when you cut claws in which the quick is not visible. If you have any doubts about being able to cut your dog's claws, have your veterinarian or petshop do it periodically.

CARE OF THE AGED DOG

With the increased knowledge and care available, there is no reason why your dog should not live to a good old age. As the years go by he may need a little additional care. Remember that an excessively fat dog is not healthy, particularly as he grows older, so limit the older dog's food accordingly. He needs exercise as much as ever, although his heart cannot bear the strain of sudden and violent exertion. Failing eyesight or hearing means lessened awareness of dangers, so you must protect him more than ever.

Should you decide at this time to get a puppy, to avoid being without a dog when your old friend is no longer with you, be very careful how you introduce the puppy. He naturally will be playful and will expect the older dog to respond to his advances. Sometimes the old dog will get a new lease on life from a new puppy, but he may be consumed with jealousy. Do not give the newcomer the attention that formerly was exclusively the older dog's. Feed them apart, and show your old friend that you still love him the most; the puppy, not being accustomed to individual attention, will not mind sharing your love.

9. Showing

There is no greater pleasure for the owner than showing a beautiful dog perfectly groomed and trained for the show ring. Whether he wins or not, it is gratifying to show a dog in superb condition, one that is a credit to your training and care. A great deal of preparation, both for you and your dog, is needed before the day that you do any serious winning. Showing is not so easy as it looks, even if you have a magnificent dog. He must be presented to the judge so that all of his good points are shown to advantage. This requires practice in gaiting, daily grooming from puppyhood, and the proper diet to make him sound in body.

When you buy your puppy you probably will think he is the best in the country and possibly in the world, but before you enter the highly competitive world of dog shows, get some unbiased expert opinion. As your dog matures, compare him with the standard of his breed. Visit a few dog shows as a spectator and make mental notes of what is required of the handlers and dogs. Watch how the experienced handlers manage their dogs to bring out their best points.

TYPES OF DOG SHOWS

There are various types of dog shows. The American Kennel Club sanctioned matches are shows at which purebred dogs may compete, but not for championship points. These are excellent for you to enter to accustom you and your dog to showing. If your dog places in a few match shows, then you might seriously consider entering the big-time shows. An American Kennel Club all-breed show is one at which purebred dogs compete for championship points. An American Kennel Club specialty show is for one breed only. It may be held in conjunction with an all-breed show (by designating the classes at that show as its specialty show) or it may be held entirely apart. Obedience trials are different in that in them the dog is judged according to his obedience and ability to perform, not by his conformation to the breed standard.

There are two types of championship conformation shows: *benched* and *unbenched*. At a benched show your dog must be on his appointed bench during the advertised hours of the show's duration. He may be removed from the bench only to be taken to the exercise pen or to be groomed (an hour before showing) in an area designated for handlers to set up their crates and grooming tables. At an unbenched show your car may serve as a bench for your dog.

To become a champion your dog must win fifteen points in competition with other dogs; a portion of the fifteen points must be awarded as major point wins (three to five points) under different judges.

HOW TO ENTER

If your dog is purebred and registered with the AKC — or eligible for registration — you may enter him in the appropriate show class for which his age, sex, and previous show record qualify him. You will find coming shows listed in the different dog magazines or at your petshop. Write to the secretary of the show, asking for the premium list. When you receive the entry form, fill it in carefully and send it back with the required entry fee. Then, before the show, you should receive your exhibitor's pass, which will admit you and your dog to the show. Here are the five official show classes:

PUPPY CLASS: Open to dogs at least six months and not more than twelve months of age. Limited to dogs whelped in the United States and Canada.

NOVICE CLASS: Open to dogs six months of age or older that have never won a first prize in any class other than the puppy class, and less than three first prizes in the novice class itself. Limited to dogs whelped in the United States or Canada.

BRED BY EXHIBITOR CLASS: Open to all dogs, except champions, six months of age or over which are exhibited by the same person, or his immediate family, or kennel that was the recognized breeder on the records of the American Kennel Club.

AMERICAN-BRED CLASS: Open to dogs that are not champions, six months of age or over, whelped in the United States after a mating which took place in the United States.

OPEN CLASS: Open to dogs six months of age or over, with no exceptions.

In addition there are local classes, the Specials Only class, and brace and team entries.

For full information on dog shows, read the book *HOW TO SHOW YOUR OWN DOG,* by Virginia Tuck Nichols. (T.F.H.)

ADVANCED PREPARATION

Before you go to a show your dog should be trained to gait at a trot beside you, with head up and in a straight line. In the ring you will have to gait your dog around the edge with other dogs and then individually up and down the center runner. In addition the dog must stand for examination by the judge, who will look at him closely and feel his head and body structure. He should be taught to stand squarely, hind feet slightly back, head up on the alert. Showing requires practice training sessions in advance. Get a friend to act as judge and set the dog up and "show" him a few minutes every day.

Sometime before the show, give your dog a bath so he will look his best. Get together all the things you will need to take to the show. You will want to take a water dish and a bottle of water for your dog (so he won't be affected by a change in drinking water). Take your show lead, bench chain (if it is a benched show), combs and brush, and the identification ticket sent by the show superintendent, noting the time you must be there and the place where the show will be held, as well as the time of judging.

THE DAY OF THE SHOW

Don't feed your dog the morning of the show, or give him at most a light meal. He will be more comfortable in the car on the way, and will show more enthusiastically. When you arrive at the show grounds, find out where he is to be benched and settle him there. Your bench or stall number is on your identification ticket, and the breed name will be on placards fastened to the ends of the row of benches. Once you have your dog securely fastened to his stall by a bench chain (use a bench crate instead of a chain if you prefer), locate the ring where your dog will be judged (the number and time of showing will be on the program of judging which came with your ticket). After this you may want to take your dog to the exercise ring to relieve himself, and give him a small drink of water. Your dog will have been groomed before the show, but give him a final brushing just before going into the show ring. When your breed judging is called, it is your responsibility to be at the ringside ready to go in. The steward will give you an armband which has on it the number of your dog.

Then, as you step into the ring, try to keep your knees from knocking! Concentrate on your dog and before you realize it you'll be out again, perhaps back with the winners of each class for more judging and finally, with luck, it will be over and you'll have a ribbon and trophy — and, of course, the most wonderful dog in the world.

BIBLIOGRAPHY

PS-606 DOLLARS IN DOGS, by Leon F. Whitney, D.V.M. The 26 chapters of this beautifully useful book tell you—frankly and clearly—how you can make money in the dog field. Every avenue to profit through dogs is explored thoroughly by Dr. Whitney, famous veterinarian and breeder. There are no punches pulled in the discussions of money-making opportunities available to everyone who wants to profit through his connection with canines. A real career-builder, 254 pages of solid and practical information, illustrated.
ISBN #0-87666-290-4
8½ x 5½ 255 pages 60 black & white photos

PS-684 DOG HOROSCOPE—YOUR DOG NEEDS A BIRTH-DAY. Probably the most clever and entertaining dog book ever published. Illustrated in color, readers are in for 64 pages of informative amusement, and you don't have to be an astrology fan to enjoy it.
ISBN #0-87666-317-X
8 x 5½ 64 pages 14 line illustrations

PS-607 HOW TO SHOW YOUR OWN DOG, by Virginia Tuck Nichols, paves the highroad to success in the fascinating and steadily growing avocation of exhibiting dogs. All of the intricacies of the show ring are explained in detail, coupled with wonderfully explicit treatments of the basics of dog shows; terms and definitions, how a champion is made, getting ready for the show, AKC rules and regulations, etc. Plus a bonus chapter on the tricks of the trade. In all, 254 well-illustrated pages that make winning in the dog show ring easier and a lot more fun.
ISBN #0-87666-390-0
8 ½ x 5½ 254 pages 136 black & white photos 10 line illustrations

H-925 DOG BREEDERS' HANDBOOK, by Ernest H. Hart. Here is the most complete and authoritative book on breeding ever written. In layman's language it clarifies all areas of this very necessary but often misunderstood subject. Beautifully presented and authored by a professional writer and recognized dog authority, the written word is augmented by profuse and pertinent illustrations.
ISBN #0-87666-286-6
85 black & white photos 12 line illustrations

PS-644 HOW TO TRAIN YOUR DOG, by Ernest H. Hart. Any dog is a better dog when well-trained. With the help of this book, any owner can do a first class job of training his dog. Fully and completely illustrated, the author takes you step by advancing step through the various areas of training. Many vital new concepts of training are advanced and discussed in this invaluable book. Color and black and white illustrations.
ISBN #0-87666-284-X
8½ x 5½ 107 pages 95 black & white photos 31 color photos

H-934 DOG OWNER'S ENCYCLOPEDIA OF VETERINARY MEDICINE, by Dr. Allan Hart. Here is a book that will become, next to his pet itself, the truest friend a dog-owner has. Page after page and chapter after chapter of valuable, pertinent information that allows an owner to make sure that his pet is given the best of care at all times. Easy to read yet brilliantly informative, this big book is a must.
ISBN #0-87666-287-4
8 x 5½ 186 pages 61 black & white photos 25 line illustrations